The Disorganized Mind

The Disorganized Mind

Coaching Your ADHD Brain to Take Control of Your Time, Tasks, and Talents

Nancy A. Ratey, Ed.M., M.C.C., S.C.A.C.

St. Martin's Griffin
New York

The circumstances and experiences described in this book are all drawn
from the author's work as an ADHD coach over the past fifteen years.
The names and other identifying characteristics of clients and their
family members have been changed to respect their privacy.

Some of the material in this book has appeared, in different format, in
Clinician's Guide to Adult ADHD Assessment and Intervention, edited by
Sam Goldstein and Anne Teeter Ellison (Academic Press, 2002).

www.stmartins.com

Book design by Mary A. Wirth

Library of Congress Cataloging-in-Publication Data

Ratey, Nancy A., 1960–
   The disorganized mind : coaching your ADHD brain to take control of your
time, tasks, and talents / Nancy A. Ratey. — 1st St. Martin's Griffin ed.
       p. cm.
   Includes index.
   ISBN-13: 978-0-312-35534-0
   ISBN-10: 0-312-35534-3
   1. Attention-deficit disorder in adults—Popular works. 2. Personal coach-
ing. I. Title.
   RC394.A85R38 2009
   616.85'89—dc22

                                                          2008042225

10 9 8 7 6 5

THIS BOOK IS IN MEMORY OF

My father
Clair William Young (8/30/1924–5/7/2004)

No matter what, you never lost hope, and you always believed in me.
Your determination and perseverance in helping me taught
me to never give up. Your spirit lives on!

My best friend
Cara Dunne-Yates (3/17/1970–10/20/2004)

Your immense love for life, laughter, and adventure was
a source of great strength and joy to me. You were the
ultimate teacher of how to live in the moment and
not sweat the small stuff. I miss you greatly.

My colleague in arms
Laura Whitworth, MCC (10/15/1947–2/28/2007)

Thank you for sharing a vision with me. We did it!
Your gift of being able to "hold the space" allowed me
to always keep my eye on the bigger picture
for that vision to grow.

Contents

Acknowledgments

I am blessed and humbled to do the work I do. To each and every one of my clients, thank you for letting me into your lives. It is an honor and privilege to have been part of your journey. Were it not for your courage to step forward, to put your trust in me, and to share your pain, struggles, and triumphs, there would be no book.

I especially thank those clients and colleagues who shared their insights with me as I planned and wrote this book.

Ned Hallowell, the field of ADHD coaching would not exist were it not for you. You saw the missing link, the way to fill the gap, to create a way for individuals with ADHD to live a more fulfilling life on a day-to-day basis. It was coaching.

Sue Sussman, I am forever indebted to you for opening the door and taking that leap of faith with me to create the National Coaching Network. It was your vision that breathed life into coaching. And to Bonnie Favorite, for helping to give shape and form to our initial training model so we could share coaching with the world, thank you.

Madelyn Griffith-Haynie and Eric Kohner, your pioneering efforts set the stage for ADHD coaching. Thank you for your tireless efforts and for helping to pave the way for coaching to become what it is today.

Also, thank you to ADDA and CHADD for your years of support for the concept of ADHD coaching.

There are many people who either directly or indirectly supported me in giving birth to this book. I thank each of you for your contributions. Thank you to Faith Hamlin, my agent; Sheila Curry Oakes, my editor at St. Martin's Press; Whitney Barrows, my "Sancho Panza"; Sherry Lowry, a wonderful coach; Joe Blackmore, Gordon Curtis, Sam Goldstein, Jackie Grupe, Ben Hillyard, Pat and Peter Latham, Karen Lu, Theresa Maitland, Terry Matlen, Rich Mintzer, Kathleen Nadeau, Patty Quinn, Sally Snowman, Dean and Sari Solden, Robert Tudisco, and Renee Van Notten.

One of the most difficult aspects of writing this book was sustaining the energy it demanded, something that would have been insurmountable without the support, encouragement, and love of my family, friends, and colleagues. Thank you all for being there when I needed you and for contributing your memories, insights, and words.

The process of writing a book is difficult to explain. It certainly takes a lot out of the person writing it, but I think it takes an equal toll on the person's family. From Ohio, Michigan, and Brazil, mine reached out to me here in Boston on a regular basis, cheering me on. To each of you, I offer love and continued thanks for the encouragement you gave to me through it all.

I am eternally grateful to my mother, June Young, whose enduring love and support have been my wings. Thank you for teaching me to laugh and for laughing with me, still.

To my friend and writer, Maureen Ackerman, thank you for giving voice to my experiences and for letting your imagination and belief in possibility inform the pages of this book.

And to my husband, John, there are no words to express how much I appreciate your steadfastness. None of this would have been possible without your unwavering love, patience, support, and expertise. You teach me, always, what "I love you" means.

Foreword

by John J. Ratey, M.D.

In the late 1980s, when Ned Hallowell and I were first refining our ideas about ADHD that led to our three *Distraction* books, we realized that when working with our adult ADHD patients, we were doing something different from simply exploring the past with these patients in an attempt to change their futures. We were doing neither classical psychotherapy nor basic diagnosis and drug treatment. Our work was different from therapy and could be done by someone who had enough training and awareness of what ADHD was all about. Ned coined the term *ADD coaching*—we called it ADD back then—and he wrote about this in *Driven to Distraction*.

About that time, Nancy and I married. I became aware that coaching was already happening in the treatment of dyslexia and that Nancy was a natural coach. She soon teamed up with Susan Sussman to combine their experiences and thoughts into a formalized curriculum to teach others how to coach adults with ADHD.

Since that time, I have come to understand and appreciate more about what ADHD is in the brain and what coaching offers in response to this type of brain difference. One of the biggest problems for patients with ADHD is that they cannot sustain the motivation to accomplish their goals, even when they have the talent and skill to do so. This fact generates many of the pejorative labels that those with ADHD accrue; they are seen as lazy, inept, and undependable. In brain lingo, the coach acts as an external frontal cortex of the left hemisphere, or specifically the executive functioning brain area, helping the individual to maintain arousal and remember motivation to succeed.

Most individuals with ADHD eventually learn that they need something to help them gain control over their lives, and those who come looking for help are, at various levels, ready to change. As a psychiatrist, I work with my patients on therapeutic issues, diagnosing and fine-tuning their medications. Often, however, as these issues are being worked on, some of the daily living issues persist. When patients are at the point of really wanting to tackle these issues and become masters of their own lives, they seek out the service of a coach to move forward on their own.

Time and time again, I've seen how Nancy helps her clients acknowledge their difficulties and begin to develop what I have called "the militant vigilance" that is so necessary to deal with their deficits. The relationship, as it is in any generative relationship focusing on personal growth, is highlighted in Nancy's work with clients. Changing the brain is hard, but you can teach an old dog new tricks, and the kind of humor-filled bond that develops between Nancy and her clients helps to cement and further their attempts at changing.

Coaching works at many levels. The relationship helps by increasing arousal and alertness in the accountability and obligations that set up what I call "good guilt." ADHD clients are often overwhelmed with guilt and shame at not fulfilling what they know they can do. But in Nancy's evolved system, clients learn to set their goals and identify that which they wish to become without the guilt and shame frequently associated with ADHD.

The coaching experience also helps the ADHD brain forgo

immediate gratification and keep in mind the concept of future reward. If individuals with ADHD could hold on to the motive, remember the consequences, and keep the reward in mind, they could move forward toward completing tasks and meeting goals. Rather than maintaining focus on a distant goal, however, the ADHD brain's attention is typically grabbed by anything that is stimulating at that moment. They can't start, they can't stay with it, they do not have the time right, and they lose focus when the frustration levels are too great or they literally have forgotten their motivation. A coach is the remedy for many of these troubles, some of which can also be helped by medication.

The coach represents cohesion for the ADHD brain, which has little experience with consistency. Coach and client work together to develop a sense of the future and the idea of being "goal-oriented." Most important, the coach reminds the client about motivation and rewards, thereby helping to avoid the old guilt associated with failure. Working with and reporting to a coach establishes a challenge and creates stimulation to reach the goal.

Sharing patients with Nancy and observing her over the years as she's worked with her clients to help them become their own executive have demonstrated to me that her coaching principles really work. In the relationship with Nancy, her clients are continually reminded of their long-term mission and goals. She gets them to focus and stay on track. Her strategies help them learn to set up their environment in the right way, so they can corral their attention through their own actions and become more productive.

The brain is amazingly plastic, and we learn anything new by changing the brain so that rewiring occurs. Eventually, the more practice that individuals with ADHD have structuring, planning, and anticipating ADHD-like troubles, the more they are training their brain to develop new habits. They become more effective themselves, and propelled by success to do even more, they move to self-coaching, incorporating the model of the coach and using it as an internal memory to achieve self-regulation and mastery of their lives.

Call me biased, if you will, for suggesting that the insights Nancy has gained from her personal journey might be reason enough for readers to trust her methodology in compensating for the symptoms of ADHD. But Nancy's perspective is broader and deeper than what she knows from living with her own ADHD. Through her years of experience coaching others with the disorder, she has seen firsthand that people can change their lives. The book demonstrates the power of coaching and/or self-coaching and the difference it can make for those with ADHD.

PART I

Coaching

"Who are you, and what do you love?" a close friend once asked me. I'm outgoing and talkative by nature, and I'm rarely at a loss for words, but I was stunned into silence by my friend's question. I had no idea how to respond.

"Don't worry," she said, sensing my discomfort. "I didn't expect you to answer. I only wanted you to imagine the possibilities of who you might be."

It's hard to know what different roads any of us might have traveled had we early on imagined our lives shaped by our loves, by our bone-deep passions and beliefs. But I don't think that *when* we begin to imagine is what matters. What matters is that it happens finally, that we come to believe such a life is possible, and that we determine, at last, to live it.

It has been awhile since my friend posed her question, and I've thought about her words a lot. Today I can answer confidently, "I'm Nancy Ratey, and I love the same things that most of us love: family, friends, some modicum of personal success."

But I can also answer another way: "I'm Nancy Ratey, life coach, and I love that the ADHD that once might have devastated me has translated into my life's passion and work: helping others with ADHD cope."

This is a book about possibility for those struggling with the symptoms of ADHD. It's about the possibility of taking control, of maintaining control, of loving the way that you live. It's about how I did it, and it's about my belief that you can do it, too.

CHAPTER 1

How I Came to Coaching

"Nancy! When are you ever going to learn from your mistakes?"

Decades later, I can still hear my father's voice, a frustrated cry of accusation and plea as he turned toward my stammering self. I had left a crayon in the pocket of my best white pants, and now the pants, and my father's white underwear, had turned a perfect pink in the wash. I had done so many things like it before, and both of us knew I would do them again. In retrospect, I can't blame my father for the things he often said.

Although I would never have admitted it as a child, I was fortunate to have been brought up in a strict and structured home. Looking back, I have no idea how my parents did it. I was the last of their four children, the oldest of whom was twelve when I was born, and I was three when they began moving us back and forth across several continents, all in conjunction with my father's work and all within a ten-year span. Clearly, someone had to take hold of the reins if we were to function as a family, and my father, a passionate and loving man of German heritage, seemed perfectly suited for the task.

Maybe he had come to his role in the family naturally, or maybe it was his background in academia and the military that had shaped his intractable ways, but the value my father placed on order and structure was evident in everything he did. My friends likened my home to a military boot camp, where we observed daily routines and abided by the strictest codes of conduct. There were time limits for almost every activity imaginable: the two-minute phone call, the three-minute shower, the thirty-minute meal.

Not one of us was spared our individual trials. My brother, Jed, always as slow as the turtles he collected, could never make it out of the house on time to catch the school bus, so my father developed a routine to get him moving. Stopwatch in hand, Dad timed Jed repeatedly while he dressed for school, packed his backpack, and walked to the bus stop. Then Dad conducted the drill: Do it once, return and repeat, do it again, return and repeat, over and over, time after time, day after day, until at last Jed was able to meet the requirement of Dad's clock.

Soon after I'd turned twelve, one of my daily chores was sweeping the kitchen floor. "Stop!" he yelled, after he'd been observing me for a while. "Watch what you're doing. The angle of the broom is all wrong." Determined to demonstrate a more efficient way to get the job done, he came over to me, tilting the broom at a sharper angle and moving my arms along with it. "See?" he said. "If you hold the broom this way, you get more dirt per sweep and you don't have to work as hard. And look, you'll get the job done faster."

From then on, no ordinary task would ever be the same, becoming instead more like a puzzle to be solved than a job to be endured. I'm not sure why I didn't hear my father's words as criticism the way my siblings and my friends did. It's enough to know that something clicked in me, and it has stayed with me ever since, influencing the way I react to others' remarks and shaping, in turn, how I speak to them. I can see now that I was learning something about listening, about processing others' comments as feedback to be considered rather than as judgment to be taken to heart.

But that's an observation I am making as an adult. As a child, all the listening in the world couldn't cure the stuttering for which I was teased and the math problems I never could solve, so I struggled through special remedial classes, misbehaving often, but managing to accomplish what would have been impossible without my father's intervention: I graduated from high school with honors. True to form, my father had designed a tight schedule for me, with specific blocks of time for each piece of homework, and to make sure that I'd stay at attention, he would check in on me often—what seemed like every five minutes to my impatient young mind—without fail, and with his trademark tap on the table to keep me on task.

I didn't know it as it was happening, of course, but through all those rituals I was also learning about structure and accountability, concepts that would serve me later in life and ultimately become the basis of some of my coaching principles. My father was making me use my brain, and he was helping me analyze what I was doing and why.

The Diagnosis

Whatever stability I might have lost as a child traveling back and forth overseas was easily offset by what I gained. Living in and learning about other cultures while I also learned their languages shaped my ability to understand a multitude of people without prejudice or judgment. The constant during all those years was my father, whose sense of order and discipline set parameters within which I could thrive.

But left to my own devices at The Ohio State University, I was lost, with a litany of reasons why. I could never get to class on time. I had no defined curriculum. I spent hours preparing to study yet never got around to actually studying. When I did sit down, I either shuffled papers for hours, not knowing what to

start working on first, or jumped from one thing to another, ultimately accomplishing nothing. It seemed as though I knew what
had to be done, but I could never get around to doing it, even
when I stayed up all night in desperation. My frustration was
deep, for sure, but it was probably equaled by that of my profes-
sors, who could not understand how someone they described as
verbal and bright would be late turning in every paper or would
perform so poorly on tests. Something was obviously amiss, one
told me. He suggested a different kind of test. This one revealed
dyslexia.

"What's in a Name?"

"Give me a name," one of my colleagues once told me about the
sudden swelling in her legs, "and at least I'll know what I'm up
against. Then I can figure out how to deal with it."

Hearing that I wasn't stupid, that I wasn't really the "space
cadet" my siblings had labeled me, I could begin to contemplate
the possibilities of a wider world. Immediately, I took advantage
of accommodations made by the university for students with
dyslexia, and my performance improved dramatically, partly because of my own efforts and partly because of my father's continued monitoring at the weekly lunches we'd arrange. A few years
later, buoyed by degrees in international relations, Portuguese,
and Spanish, I headed off to Cambridge, Massachusetts, where I
worked for eight months as a foreign student adviser to candi-
dates in the master's degree in public policy program before the
position folded and the increasing confidence with which I had
headed east slowly evaporated.

For two years I was unemployed, unable to keep even a hand-
ful of temporary jobs. In one sense, my employers were right
about my shortcomings: I did misfile papers; I did cross phone
lines as a receptionist; I really couldn't type or spell. But those

problems notwithstanding, I truly believed I had much to offer. I had grown up on three different continents, and I spoke several languages. I also had useful analytical and people skills. Yet to a prospective employee, that rich life experience could not compensate for either my inability to do basic administrative work or my obvious challenges in reading and writing.

It has been more than twenty years since those dark days in Cambridge, and sometimes I still wonder if something else had been hovering just below the surface of potential employers' minds. At the time, it seemed there were more misconceptions than facts about dyslexia, and I often felt I was the target of silent discrimination because I was so open about my own. My diagnosis was double-edged. It made available to me services that helped me succeed, even as it prompted work-related doubts that I actually could.

At Harvard

Going to Harvard changed my life, but not for the obvious reasons. Few, if any, would have predicted that I'd earn a graduate degree, especially those remedial high school teachers who had often assigned me detention. But given my wandering attention and inability to sit still, neither would they have been surprised at the difficulties I experienced before I had the degree in hand.

As a proud student in the master's degree program in administration, planning, and social policy at the Harvard Graduate School of Education, I wanted to be a model of excellence, completing my work on time and earning the grades my effort and preparation would deserve. I was deluding myself. Instead of the success I was envisioning, I experienced the all-too-familiar setbacks of the past. Like a tourist without a map on foreign terrain, I wandered through a setting without structure, seeing where I needed to go but unable to follow the road to get there. I was crushed.

Countless therapists and psychiatrists later, I was given a name for the symptoms I was exhibiting and, with that name, a way to understand my brain and what I might do to harness it. I was tested yet again, I was diagnosed yet again, and with medication that I was subsequently prescribed for the attention deficit hyperactivity disorder (ADHD) the doctors discovered, I began to develop the self-awareness to know when I was getting off track.

Because I had learned what was wrong, I could also learn how to make the situation right. For the first time in my life, I found the missing link between desire and actual performance as I created strategies for studying and a sense of structure that would allow me to succeed. And for the second time in my life, it was the diagnosis—the name—that made the difference in how I'd proceed.

Beyond the Classroom

As I began to devise methods to keep myself on top of studying at Harvard, I was also driven by a desire to prevent others from experiencing the problems that I had faced in both school and the workplace. To raise awareness of dyslexia and ADHD, I began a speaker series that would eventually run for eight years and which not only encouraged students to seek accommodations from the administration, but also shaped how Harvard viewed students with learning disabilities and ADHD. I quickly became a spokesperson for students in higher education with learning disabilities and in 1988 I was invited to testify before a United States congressional committee on behalf of persons with learning disabilities to help implement the Americans with Disabilities Act (ADA).

As a result of my increasing visibility, others began to seek my advice on how to self-manage, and I found myself passing on to them all the early lessons from my father that I had incorporated into my life, especially *structure, accountability,* and *partnership.* Meeting with them regularly for lunch and dinner, as my father had met with me during my undergraduate days, I monitored their progress and discussed their follow-through on commitments they had made to themselves. Time and again, they told me how amazed they were at the successes they began to achieve. I was amazed, too, but more by the role I was playing, I think, than by the results they were enjoying. I had grown up, after all, learning lessons of accountability, and I knew firsthand what a sense of structure might mean. What I hadn't realized before was that I could give to others the gifts my father had given me.

"A Coach by Any Other Name . . ."

"Look what you're doing here," my husband, John J. Ratey, psychiatrist and associate professor of psychiatry at Harvard Medical School, said to me one afternoon after yet another acquaintance had checked in with me by phone. "You're coaching!"

The informal work I had been doing with ADHD students and staff members at Harvard had led to more formal support groups with ADHD professionals, and some of those had begun to request one-on-one appointments with me. Sometimes we'd meet for lunch, other times we'd speak on the phone, and occasionally we'd correspond by e-mail. How we communicated didn't really matter, though, for the outcome of our talking remained consistent. By taking control of various aspects of their lives, those who had sought my advice were accomplishing more and enjoying life more than they had previously imagined possible. And I was helping them to get where they wanted to be, as excited as they were through every step of the journey.

My husband had been right. My own struggles with ADHD, the childhood lessons of structure and self-discipline imparted by my father, and the innate exuberance and energy that informed my work with others had led my husband to the observation that would define my existence from that point on: I was coaching! I was talking to clients! At once, I could envision the rest of my life!

Another name. Another life-altering moment. Another word to add to my personal lexicon.

Collaboration

Once I began my first real work with clients, I was on a mission to understand just why and how coaching works so well for individuals with ADHD, and I often shared clients with my husband, who specializes in the diagnosis and treatment of ADHD. John, the psychiatrist, would concentrate on the medical and therapeutic issues of our clients, and I would help them with concrete, day-to-day matters. We'd spend hours analyzing and discussing the impact coaching was having on the clients' lives, and as we considered the brain's functioning, we were able to fine-tune our understanding of the specific role the coach played from a practical, as well as neuropsychiatric, perspective.

Coaches, we saw, allow clients to compensate for their brain differences by helping them design strategies individualized for their respective needs. We also saw that coaches serve as external checks on clients' internal inconsistencies, partnering with clients in discovering ways to succeed.

Basically, the interplay between ADHD coaching and ADHD clients works like this:

PEOPLE WITH ADHD TYPICALLY NEED HELP IN THESE AREAS:
- Considering consequences before acting on a thought
- Setting goals and prioritizing
- Keeping a goal in mind
- Sequencing out steps toward a goal

- Directing attention to the task at hand
- Creating and sticking to timelines
- Keeping track of time
- Staying focused
- Keeping thoughts at bay
- Not blurting out feelings

COACHING HELPS CLIENTS IN THESE AREAS:
- Time management
- Organizational skills
- Establishing priorities
- Building self-acceptance
- Building self-esteem
- Mastering interpersonal skills and techniques
- Self-monitoring

As I learned more about the brain and the behavioral aspects of ADHD, I was able to clarify my understanding of the role of the coach in a client's life and hone my own coaching skills as well. I saw that the *partnership* aspect of coaching accounted for most of the clients' success, specifically because as I provided support, encouragement, and expertise, they learned how to recognize and address particular problems they were experiencing. The goal was to prepare clients for independence and self-management.

COACHING HELPS YOU CREATE "GOOD STRESS"

"Forget standing at the edge of the cliff," one client remarked about his own need for increased intensity in order to get himself focused. "I need to be standing *on the blade!*"

People with ADHD often need a certain level of stress in order to achieve a goal. To give them the feeling of urgency they need, the sense that "I'm out of time here, so I have to get this done," I work with my clients to create interim deadlines and schedules, and I arrange phone check-ins to keep them on pace. Essentially, I'm helping my clients create the "good stress" they need to reach their goals. Ultimately, they learn how to create that functional level of urgency for themselves.

COACHING HELPS YOU CHANGE EMOTIONAL RESPONSES

People with ADHD are often plagued by shame and guilt, and "I'm sorry" is a programmed response.

Part of my coaching responsibility is to help my clients identify negative feelings and the many things that trigger them so they can control their emotional responses. "You are not your ADHD," I remind them over and again. "You can change that behavior by implementing certain strategies." The goal is that they stop blaming themselves. By stepping back and looking objectively at what they are doing, they can identify the ADHD source of their behavior and initiate necessary change.

I've seen how a coach can instill hope in the client who, left alone with years of negative voices playing inside the head, might readily give up in the face of tasks that seem overwhelming. I've also seen how that hope can be a catalyst for action.

COACHING HELPS YOU STAY MOTIVATED

People with ADHD are often judged as lacking in motivation, but a coach can help change the self-image perpetuating that myth. I like to remind my clients of the gains they have made, and I've seen how that kind of encouragement can bolster their self-confidence. They can allow themselves to feel good when I affirm their success, which then gives them increased motivation to follow through on systems they know are working. There's nothing like success to breed more success!

COACHING HELPS YOU SELF-INITIATE CHANGE

In order to function autonomously, we must be able to screen out distractions, sustain attention, and use feedback appropriately, all of which are chronic problems for many individuals with ADHD.

To compensate for these deficits, I help my clients observe themselves in action, a necessary step in becoming aware of what they are doing *while they are actually doing it.* Eventually, they develop the ability to take charge of their behavior so they can act rather than react.

For individuals with ADHD, then, coaching can be the difference between minimal functioning and true, full living. Clients can learn how to eliminate the frustration they often feel from their ADHD by understanding their own brains and adjusting their actions accordingly. In small increments, they can begin to make significant changes, until they feel in control of their ADHD symptoms. Ideally, they can learn to live more fulfilling, satisfying lives.

One of the most powerful gifts my father gave me was the ability to analyze. More specifically, he trained me to analyze my own actions and behaviors, the ones that I was always repeating and that simultaneously got me into trouble.

Because this ability to analyze required skills of observation, my father was training me at the same time to observe myself in action—*to become aware of what I was doing as I was doing it*—so I could answer the questions that he continually posed, the same ones I later learned to ask of myself: "What can you do to prevent this in the future?" "What strategies can you use?" "What can you anticipate will get in your way?" "How will you know when you are getting off track?"

I can certainly admit that it was no fun being accountable to my father for my actions or lack of actions. It was no fun, either, trying to self-manage during all those years without the benefit of knowing I was struggling with ADHD. But the demands my father made on me and the questions he had me asking myself are now the hallmark of my coaching style. I like to think that I'm as dogged and caring with my clients as he was with me and that the strong commitment I require from my clients to themselves is no less than the one my father demanded of me.

Let me now ask you the question my friend asked me: Who are you, and can you live the life you love?

Coaching can help you consider how you want to answer. It encourages you to look at your lifestyle, to think about the choices you're making, and to live a life that's balanced and rich. It essentially guides you toward taking control of how you're living so you can actually love the way you live.

Talking about her own life the other day, a writer friend made an analogy to the coaching process. "Like the garden tended or the marriage nurtured," she told me, "or like the life lived with courage or the miles logged each week—none of it just *happens*. But isn't it better to know that," she went on, "or where would any of us fit in the picture of our own lives? When things work out the way you want them to, you can call it luck or a gift or even grace, but whatever you name it, you still have to use it to make it matter. You have to act! And isn't that the point—that we choose how we're going to live? That we exercise control?"

Coaching can help you attain the control that seems so elusive now, and it can help you maintain that control once you begin to make it happen.

Believe it, and you'll already have begun!

CHAPTER 2

How Coaching Works

When I was thirteen, I lived in Uganda, East Africa, where most of the learning in the school I attended was hands-on. When our class hiked up Mount Elgon on one of our many field trips, each of us was assigned a guide who would hike up the mountain with us. The guides would not say much, but they would help us carry our packs if we needed assistance or provide direction and protection when necessary by pointing out slippery spots, narrow ledges, or weak places in the bridges we had to cross. The important thing was that our guides never carried us on their backs or hiked for us. They simply stayed close by. As we learned more about what to watch out for, our guides would fall a bit behind, letting us revel in our newfound confidence and explore the paths by ourselves.

Essentially, the guides were doing what a coach does. A coach will help you recognize and maneuver around the obstacles in your way, waiting there in the shadows while you develop your own skills and strategies to reach your goal. A coach will stay with you, but a coach will not walk for you.

Athletes, musicians, and business professionals have known the value of coaching for years. They hire coaches to help them discover and focus on what works for them so they can reach the goals they've set. They recognize that the coaching partnership can make all the difference between satisfactory performance and maximum performance, and those who are tops in their respective fields have obviously opted for the latter.

I suppose it's easy to understand, then, how personal coaching has become so widespread among the general population. Living in a culture of quick-fix expediency and instant gratification, and faced with increasingly burdensome demands on their time and attention, people are searching for ways to deal with the overload they feel while still trying to make choices that fulfill and honor who they are.

One problem I've seen is that many don't really know who they are, and they don't have any idea how to begin finding out. What I've learned as a coach is that most people simply haven't thought about the kind of life they want to live before they're caught up in living it. Somehow, they say, they've landed in a job or a relationship or a situation without understanding how they got there. "I feel lost," they tell me. "I just don't know what I'm doing. How could this have happened?"

Personal coaching helps people focus on understanding their own needs, and it teaches them to set goals for changing old behavior patterns and creating new ones. In my role, I provide a supportive place from which my clients can examine their lives as I ask them to consider, perhaps for the very first time, that intriguing question that stunned me into silence: Who are you?

Even more, I permit them, perhaps also for the first time, to consider the possibilities inherent in the answer. Most of us, it seems, are so accustomed to the etiquette of putting ourselves last, of not being or appearing self-absorbed, that we feel guilty even considering our own needs. It's selfish, we think. It's not loving or kind or good. The personal coach asks you to change the focus and look inward, not for its own sake, not to foster selfish behavior, but to manage a life that too often feels out of control.

Discovering Strategies for Success

In essence, I try to create a climate of support and encouragement so my clients can discover for themselves how to replace
negative, defeating behaviors with positive patterns for success.
David, for example, had trouble paying bills on time, not because
he didn't have adequate funds in his checking account, but because he thought he could write the checks one Saturday a
month rather than once a week. It would be easier, he insisted, to
let all the bills accumulate and to take care of them at one sitting.
The problem was that he was then left with an insurmountable
pile, so he'd turn toward biking or photography or anything else
he considered a more pleasurable activity than check writing,
while his bills incurred late charges.

My job was not to agree with David's judgment that he was
"being irresponsible" and that he was "throwing money away." It
was to listen to what he thought was wrong, remind him of the
importance of paying his bills, and guide him toward how he
wanted me to help him remember the consequences of paying
late—that he was being charged extra money each month, money
that could have been spent on better things. Through our work
together, he laid out a plan to address his bills weekly and let me
know how he wanted me to hold him accountable.

When I talked with David about how he wanted me to respond
when he saw that he wasn't following through, he realized that
what he had initially decided—that I should just excuse his lack
of commitment and ask him to try again the next week—wasn't
working. After discussing different approaches I might try in its
place, he decided on a new strategy that helped him accomplish
the original task. He paid the bills on time and as a bonus had all
that former late charge money to use however he wanted!

This is the power of ADHD coaching. First you assess your
most pressing needs. Then you apply strategies to address them,

fine-tuning with the coach until you get the results you need and growing ever more confident that they'll stick because you've come up with them yourself. Having invested so much of yourself in the planning, after all, you really want the plan to succeed, which is what motivates you to work hard at making it happen.

How ADHD Coaching Works

Just as in any coaching partnership, clients with ADHD have to be ready for the experience and willing and able to meet the challenge of creating better lives for themselves. What's different about clients with ADHD is the reason they need a coach in the first place.

Basically, ADHD coaching focuses on the unique biological differences in the ADHD brain that have caused the individual to have less control over his life than he wants and needs to have. An ADHD coach understands the neurobiological symptoms at the root of negative habits and behavior patterns and, through this recognition, helps the client learn to navigate the daily challenges caused by the symptoms.

I explain to my clients that the coaching experience is like a journey to learn more about themselves and how ADHD plays a role in their lives. It's a journey of self-discovery that helps them learn about their ADHD brain and become more effective at home, at work, and at play.

The very nature of ADHD dictates that the brain's executive function—its ability to screen out distractions, to hold things in mind, to consider consequences—is not working as well as it might. If you have ADHD, you know from experience that planning ahead, prioritizing, and following through on commitments are difficult. Simple tasks like paying the bills, getting enough sleep, taking medication consistently, and remembering to perform household chores can present as much difficulty for you as long-term, more complex work projects might for people without ADHD.

You also know that making things stick is never easy. You've probably struggled to develop new habits, but it wouldn't be surprising if you've simply given up after repeated failed attempts. No one has to tell you that you're disorganized or inconsistent, no matter how many times you've sworn not to disappoint others or yourself. You know how you are, and the fact that you're reading this book suggests that you're as frustrated by your inability to follow through as other people in your life probably are. You might have been asked "Why can't you just keep a to-do list?" more times than you care to remember. Or, "Why can't you just hang your keys on a hook so you won't lose them anymore?"

On a regular basis, my clients tell me how guilty and ashamed they feel, how incompetent and helpless they believe they are. They promise to do things differently, but then they find themselves repeating the old patterns. "I'm so sick and tired of always turning over a new leaf," Sarah, a speech pathologist, cried to me recently. "Nothing seems to work. It's like I'm stuck in the 'spin cycle' and can't seem to get out. I just feel so stupid!"

ADHD Is Not a Character Flaw

Sarah's feelings of inadequacy and frustration were understandable, but ADHD is not a character flaw. It is a neurobiological disorder that she needed to understand so that she could create strategies to address the ADHD symptoms she was exhibiting and then do what was necessary to make changes. Ridding herself of those negative feelings was certainly possible, I assured her, but I emphasized that it was up to her to learn as much as she could and then take the responsibility to adjust her life accordingly.

What Sarah could learn, for example, was that it's her ADHD brain that makes her easily sidetracked, and it's her ADHD that makes her do the same kinds of things over and over that she's consistently promised not to repeat. In time, she could also learn that she's not deliberately forgetting the consequences of prior actions and causing herself repeated pain. She's forgetting because of differences in her brain that cause her to forget. Once she was able to acknowledge that fact, she'd be able to create strategies to bring about the changes she was seeking.

The same is true for you. Your ADHD won't go away, so you need to understand it and plan for the ways it affects you. Coaching can be helpful in bridging the gap between your desire to initiate an action and your actually performing it and following it through. There's no reason you have to let new commitments or challenges slip away with your resolve. That old behavior pattern puts you at risk for losing hope and giving up.

You have to change the pattern. You have to create new strategies to address what has traditionally left you overwhelmed. You literally have to develop new habits that use the strengths of your ADHD brain so that you can succeed. Remember, most of the time you certainly know what you want to accomplish. Creative strategies that you initiate and develop through coaching can actually help you do it.

Fortunately, exciting discoveries made by neuroscientists suggest that the brain is flexible in its ability to learn continually. Rehearsing actions helps to forge new neural pathways in the brain so it can develop competencies in areas that historically have been deficient. This flexibility of the brain, with its ability to adapt, is one way new habits are learned.

Because I've seen its results, I firmly believe that coaching accomplishes two important things: It paves the pathway for this learning to occur, and it makes a real difference in how people with ADHD negotiate their particular deficits to cope with life on a daily basis. They learn to self-initiate change.

Understanding that the brain can learn provides the energy

that should help you make positive, lasting changes, as you turn an "I can't" attitude into an "I can!" attitude. A coach can serve as your cheerleader, helping you to build and maintain hope as you do the difficult work of making the changes in your life that you know you need.

Precepts of ADHD Coaching

A few years ago, one of my clients, Connie, told me that our experience working together reminded her of what she'd been striving to create for her children. Whenever she thought about growing up, she still felt her own parents' disappointment when she didn't follow through on her tasks, and she still heard the sting of disapproval when they constantly demanded to know, "What's wrong with you? Why didn't you finish your homework? How could you have lost your assignment pad?"

With her own children, Connie wanted to create conditions where they wouldn't feel judged or threatened the way she remembered feeling as a child. She was trying, in other words, to address what they might be doing without judging who they were as people. More than anything, she wanted them to be able to separate the action from the person performing the act, so they could keep their self-esteem intact.

Working with my clients, I'm conscious of creating conditions that let them succeed, and I try to offer a nonjudgmental space for them to reflect on their behavior, so I was grateful that Connie noticed the connection between what I was doing with her and what she was doing with her children. Prodding as gently yet as persistently as I can, I help my clients discover strategies for coping with the demands of their daily lives. That relentless urging has earned me the reputation of "Mother Teresa in army boots," but it's also garnered successes for my clients that have changed their lives.

The Importance of Balance

One of the most important things to understand is that coaching is fundamentally *holistic,* which means that it involves working on all aspects of your life. What you learn to understand is that lifestyle choices matter. What you eat, for example, or how much sleep you get has an effect on your daily functioning. The strength of your social network or spiritual life also affects your well-being, as does the level of satisfaction you derive from your job. Working alongside a coach, you'll develop an overall plan to address the multiple layers of your daily life by compensating for the symptoms of ADHD that interfere with living fully.

I can't stress enough with my clients how allowing one aspect of life to so dominate that it virtually excludes others—too much work, no exercise, for example—almost guarantees less than maximum functioning. Our mothers told us not to put all our eggs in one basket. Financial advisers tell us to diversify. Guidance counselors tell high school seniors that colleges are looking for well-rounded students. The language might be different, but the message is the same. We are more than our jobs, more than our circle of acquaintances, more than our transcripts and résumés, more than the golf partners of our friends.

Each one of us is an individual with a unique mind and body and spirit needing attention and care and respect. For most of us with ADHD, the question is not "Do I believe this?" but "How do I consistently translate that belief into consistent action?" In other words, "How do I stop being *consistently inconsistent?*"

I'm a runner, and I've completed several marathons, but sometimes I'm still daunted by the idea of facing more than twenty-six miles at once. Let's suppose that you wanted to take up running yourself and that you thought running with me might help you get started. Assuming that you were physically able to do so, I certainly wouldn't invite you for a five-miler the first day. I'd let you take a few beginning steps, though, I'd talk to you about a strategy to increase how far you'd eventually be able to go, and I'd emphasize the importance of the shorter distances that ultimately become the longer ones. I'd break your runs down into segments you could manage, and I'd add the miles gradually.

In other words, I'd try to make sure you remained undaunted by the task at hand by laying out a strategy you could master. That thousand-mile journey really does begin with that first, and most essential, step, but there's no magic in what happens after that. It takes planning and effort and commitment to make it happen.

Most of us have probably heard athletes and sports enthusiasts talk about a particular sport as a metaphor for life itself. To be the best, the athlete has to develop all aspects of his or her game. It might be enough for a while to have the fastest serve or the purest jump shot, but one perfect skill doesn't guarantee perfect overall functioning.

Coaches help athletes concentrate on the individual skills that combine for a complete package. It's the same with ADHD coaching. A coach asks you to consider your complete lifestyle and to develop strategies to address all areas that need work. But because the notion of balance matters, the coach provides support as you carry out the plan to achieve your goals, one single, essential step at a time. Since individuals with ADHD often try to do everything at the same time, this coaching approach is important so that success remains within reach. ADHD coaches understand that setting the goals too high by trying to accomplish everything at once— which is also characteristic of the ADHD brain—sets clients up for failure by sabotaging their efforts to succeed.

The Importance of Readiness

Naturally, the question arises whether coaching can actually benefit everyone coping with ADHD. Experience has taught me that the answer lies in a potential client's *readiness*. Coaching presumes, for example, that clients are healthy, that they have an idea of what their issues are, and that they are ready to devote the time to work on them, needing the coach only to draw them out.

Because coaching is a process of exploration that takes place over a period of time, much of your success will rest on your readiness to commit both time and spirit to the endeavor.

"But how will I know I'm ready?" you might ask.

The answer isn't difficult. You'll know you're ready for coaching when you can admit that you have a problem, when you agree to spend the time necessary to create strategies to improve your behavior, and when you are willing to adhere to those strategies to the best of your ability. When you want to change, and when you agree to work hard at what's necessary, as long and as difficult a process as that might be, you're ready to begin. It's that simple.

But it's also a leap of faith. You have to believe in the possibility of change and make a commitment to seeing it through!

The ADHD Coaching Model

The possibility, even likelihood, of setbacks is inherent in any long-term process, so I have to provide encouragement, recommendations, feedback, and practical techniques to get my clients through the challenging times. A coach will help you develop strategies to address issues such as managing time, eliminating clutter in your home or office, and becoming more effective, and thereby happier, both professionally and personally.

As a coach, I can see my clients' problems within the context of their daily lives, and I indicate to them where they're likely to have trouble. But why these things happen is not our issue. I don't get into the psychological baggage they might be carrying from years ago but concentrate instead on the present and future. The question is, "What can you do about it?" or, "How can you motivate yourself to act toward your goal?" or, "When is your deadline?" I focus, in other words, on *what, how,* and *when,* questions designed to help my clients compensate for their ADHD problems by creating strategies that work for them. I concentrate on the practical details they need to address, daily.

As coach, I guide the process, I provide structure, I ask questions, and I make observations. But I do not judge or impose. If coaching is going to work, it's up to the client to drive the process forward.

Core Elements of Coaching

PARTNERSHIP

By working in partnership with the coach, you determine not only exactly what you need from coaching, but also how you'll get it. Your job is to tell the coach the areas in which you need help and then set the ground rules of the partnership so you'll succeed. David, you remember, wanted to take control of his finances so he'd not only improve his credit rating, he'd also have more discretionary money available by eliminating late charges. He decided to pay his bills weekly, and he instructed me on how to keep him on task. What's important in this process is that by telling me how he wanted to be accountable for reaching his goals, he ultimately assumed responsibility for attaining them himself.

You can enjoy a similar success. As you define and then redefine your goals, the coach will help you shape your interaction in a way that will work most effectively for your needs, all the while factoring in practical considerations that will allow you to succeed. Over time, and with your coach's assistance, you should understand more about what actually motivates you and more about what gets in your way.

The point, of course, is that the balance in the partnership eventually can shift from the coach's external reminder to your own internal voice. Ultimately, it will be that internal voice that will allow you to self-initiate change. Armed with the ability to understand both what you need to do and how you can accomplish it, you'll permit your coach to retreat further and further to the background until you can function on your own.

STRUCTURE

Within the coaching partnership, structure is one of the most vital elements, but it is also one of the most difficult for many people to accept. If you're like most of my clients, you probably have that proverbial love/hate relationship with structure. On the one hand, you feel constricted by schedules and structures that require you to perform tasks that you don't like doing. On the other hand, it's usually structure itself that makes you successful at completing those tasks, making them less threatening or unpalatable to begin with.

Working together, you and your coach will try to understand your learning style so you can develop tools that match your strengths. The goal is for you to build structures that suit your particular style, structures that work *with* your strengths and *not against* them. Maybe you don't need to lay out all your clothes the night before you'll wear them, for example, or write your whole week's shopping list in one sitting, as is necessary for somebody else. The key is to recognize the kind of structure that works for your personality and unique style and then to put that structure in place.

Structure is designed to improve your focus by taking you through the steps of *attending to details, planning, organizing, and prioritizing for your goals.* Structure is absolutely necessary in order to move forward, for without it, there's more than a good chance that you'll become distracted by your environment, opt for immediate gratification, and get off track. That's why the strategy has to work with your own style and preference.

Once he decided that paying his bills weekly was absolutely necessary, for example, David also saw that he was choosing the wrong day to do it. By nature he was someone who loved being outdoors. Of course he wanted to ride his bike rather than pay his bills on a clear and sunny Saturday!

Under the same circumstances, people without ADHD might find it difficult enough to resist the pull of clean air and open road, but for those coping with ADHD, it might be impossible to stay focused on paying the bills. David and others like him could easily forget the importance of the goal because it lacked "immediacy." Since not incurring late charges and having more money at the end of the month would not affect the specific moment in which they were living, they would be far more likely to turn to the reward of what they could grasp right then and there—in David's case, pedaling through a perfect afternoon.

Establishing structures, ones particularly suited to you, reinforces the successful behaviors and keeps you from straying off course. The idea is that the routines you establish make it possible for you to focus on what needs to be done to reach your goals. The more success you have, the more you'll be inclined to stick with what you're doing, widening your vision about what's possible for you to achieve. We all find it easier to face tasks we enjoy and that we're good at, or at least ones we know we're capable of completing.

In other words, coaching helps you lengthen your "I can!" list. As you begin to experience a sense of ownership—of being in charge of your own life—you'll become more motivated to move the experience forward. The more success you have, the more you'll want to have!

PROCESS

The third important principle of coaching is to help you develop an ability to *look inward, identify needs,* and *articulate a solution* to the perceived problems. By listening carefully and remaining emotionally detached, I pose questions in as nonjudgmental a way as possible, avoiding, for example, "Why didn't you do that?" and asking instead, "What prevented you from doing that? What choices might you have next time?"

I never asked David, "How could you have put off those bills again? Why can't I trust you to follow through?" Instead I asked him, "What did you do instead of writing those checks?"

By slowing down and listing activities that he had chosen instead of paying his bills, David recognized how he had been creating his own problem by choosing an unrealistic time to accomplish his task. He acknowledged how much biking on weekends meant to him and admitted that he didn't want to surrender that time to something he could just as easily do on a night during the week. By realizing that he was working against himself, he could establish a new routine to get the job done.

Words matter. They matter more than most people acknowledge, and for the coach, they can make all the difference in the client's success. I said earlier that my siblings and friends often heard my father's comments as criticism, but I had somehow escaped that emotional response and could zero in on the point of what my father was saying. I don't take any chances with my clients, so I'm careful to choose language that lets them concentrate on specific actions and solutions rather than on feeling guilty or irresponsible.

By modeling objective, nonthreatening language, I'm also teaching my clients how to use it on their own. Eventually, instead of thinking, "I'm such a jerk. I don't do anything right. I can't even pay my bills!" David was able to realize, "I pay the bills late because I get distracted and forget the consequences of not paying them, and I let them pile up. I need to pay them once a week. I don't want to do them on Saturday when I could be biking. I can leave a note on my desk every Monday morning to remind me to write the checks Monday night. I can set the alarm on my desk to go off at 10:00 p.m. to remind me again just in case I've forgotten."

When the focus is on solving the problem—when the discussion between you and the coach is on creating solutions rather than exploring or assigning blame—you can eventually internalize the questions and be able to process what you're doing independently.

For you to succeed, you have to believe that you can succeed. Because many people with ADHD have been misunderstood and labeled "stupid," learning to reframe their disability can make all the difference in their daily functioning. By separating yourself from the negative scripts that hold you back, you can begin to look at yourself more objectively.

That's the point of coaching: Through guided self-exploration, you designate your own problem areas, and you come up with your own solutions. You empower yourself by taking ownership and control of your actions.

What Clients Say

Many people with ADHD appear to have it all together at work but fall apart when it comes to basic tasks at home. The career woman in top form at the office often feels as if she's leading a double life, accomplishing important things at the law firm but collapsing with guilt and frustration at the laundry pile growing at home. Fortunately, no one has to accept life on those terms. Coaching can provide a different way.

I don't pretend that it's easy, but I definitely contend that it's worth the work. I know that my clients agree.

"Coaching offers something new to me, something I cannot really describe," one woman wrote about her experience. "But I had no idea how painful the process was going to be, or how rewarding. One of the first things I discovered, common among women with ADHD, is that I always had too much on my agenda for any given time period. I also had no clue how to prioritize. Whatever was most pressing at the moment, or perhaps most interesting, or required the least mental effort, was *next* on my agenda. I spent a lot of time giving in to the overwhelmed feeling this method of getting through the day gave me.

"The coach's questions are always designed to get me moving, and they're not at all threatening, but they never feel quite like rewards. When she asks, 'How are you going to get that done?' or, 'When are you going to have that completed by?' the pain I'm already feeling only gets worse. I sometimes ask myself, 'Who in their right mind would pay for this torture?' In the very next thought, though, I am always grateful that I have found someone who can get me from point A to point B without judgment and with incredible patience."

That's how ADHD coaching goes, really. It's pain and it's progress. It's forward, it's back, then it's forward again. It's the challenge and it's the reward, at once.

Many individuals with ADHD live in turmoil. It doesn't have to be that way. Remember that you have choices. Imagine how things can change. By using ADHD strategies that you create, and by learning to organize, plan, and prioritize, you'll clear the hurdles of daily living with a confidence and success you might never before have dreamed possible.

My clients have done it.

Now it's your turn to say, "I can!"

CHAPTER 3

Self-Coaching

You might say that I coach what I know, having lived it, and that I'm putting my insights to work. The fact that I can offer you this book, especially the promise that it holds for you, is based directly on my experience with ADHD, personally and professionally. I am telling you what I know to be true, which makes it easier for me to ask you to trust the coaching process.

Scan the television offerings or look around any bookstore. Self-help programs and books abound, but if what they suggest were impossible to achieve, no one would watch or read what is available. The truth is *you can help yourself*. With the right commitment, you can take responsibility for your life and coach yourself toward change and control.

Joseph, a recent client, revealed a common reason people seek out coaching. His inability to fulfill his responsibilities at home had been creating inordinate amounts of stress for his family. "My wife says she's tired of having to do everything for me," Joseph said. "She's fed up because I'm always asking her where things are or when we're supposed to do something. She says I need to learn some self-discipline about taking responsibility for things on my own."

It wasn't exactly an ultimatum that had been rendered by his wife, but Joseph knew he wasn't going to change without help.

Allan, another client, came to me because of a problem at work. A business partner had made it abundantly clear that Allan needed to manage time more efficiently or risk losing his share in the business. For both clients, and for many men and women like them, an element of desperation lay behind their initial inquiry. They were searching for control over problems that interfered with their relationships and livelihood. They sought the help of a coach because somebody important had made clear what was at stake if they didn't.

There are many reasons you might have picked up this book. You may have simply felt ready to take charge of your life, rather than responding to pressure from other people. Perhaps you're aware that there are problems in key areas of your life, but you haven't been able to figure out exactly what's wrong. Perhaps you're not even sure you have ADHD, but because you know you're not functioning as well as you want to, you sense that something within is throwing you off course. Maybe you think this book can help you understand what that is and that you can learn, at last, what to do about it. Or maybe you've been diagnosed with ADHD, and now you want to learn to compensate for your symptoms by reading about what has worked for others. There's even the possibility that you have been coached before and are now looking for reminders about staying on track.

Whatever the reason you decided to read, there are lessons in self-coaching that you can learn. The basic premise behind coaching and self-coaching is the same, after all, so the real difference will come down to the person to whom you'll be accountable. Obviously, success comes from commitment, and you have to be honest with yourself about keeping that commitment. Adults with ADHD often have a long history of self-deception, so you have to recognize from the outset that it's probably easier for you than for an objective outsider like a coach to excuse minimal effort. But if you hold yourself to the highest standards, the kind to which I learned to hold myself, then being your own coach is not only possible, it's well worth the effort involved.

First Things First

Adults with ADHD typically answer "*yes*" to certain questions about their behavior patterns. Obviously, many people exhibit some of these behaviors some of the time, but that doesn't necessarily mean that they have ADHD. The number of symptoms, the frequency of those symptoms, and the severity of those symptoms all become factors in the diagnosis of ADHD. The important thing for you to understand is that you should not attempt to diagnose yourself. The following questions are meant as a guide:

- Do you frequently feel stuck, unable to "get your act together," or unable to meet your goals?
- Do you find yourself with too many projects at once, so many that you can't follow through with any of them?
- Are you easily distracted or unable to focus?
- Is it difficult for you to get organized?
- Do you frequently procrastinate, resisting the idea of beginning your work?
- Are you frequently impulsive?
- Do you frequently speak without thinking about the consequences of your words?
- Do you forget the consequences of past actions, thereby repeating mistakes?
- Do you have problems with self-acceptance and self-esteem?
- Are you too easily bored, too easily attracted to some new stimulus?
- Do you frequently begin projects enthusiastically, only to lose interest?

If you answered "*yes*" to most of these questions, you should get an actual diagnosis to make sure that other factors are not also at work.

Many people with ADHD struggle with significant emotional issues, which should not be downplayed or ignored. A diagnosis

SEEKING A DIAGNOSIS FOR ADULT ADHD
by John J. Ratey, M.D.

NOTE: YOU SHOULD NEVER SELF-DIAGNOSE FOR ADHD

If you have been troubled by the following symptoms throughout your life, and if the symptoms are severe enough that they interfere with your daily activities and relationships, then you should visit a professional who has experience in this area: a psychiatrist, psychologist, experienced family practitioner, or other medical professional known to be expert.

COMMON SYMPTOMS OF ADULT ADHD

Persistent symptoms of the following are often found in adult ADHD:
Trouble starting and finishing projects
Trouble organizing steps in a project, paper, letter, home, office
Trouble with memory—worry about Alzheimer's since the teen years; misplacing
      things, pirouette sign (coming back and back again for something you forgot)
World-class procrastination
Internal feeling of being antsy, squirming, restless legs syndrome all throughout
      body
Difficulty focusing, paying attention during a conversation, attending lecture,
      watching movie, or reading a book
Impatient to a fault; finishing people's sentences for them, drawing rapid conclu-
      sions, or breaking into conversations; episodes of road rage or extreme temper
Distractibility, spacing out

Before visiting a medical professional, it is helpful to outline on paper your history
of attention problems, dating from childhood, including the following:
1. School performance, relationship issues, job history
2. Problems with authority, paying attention, nicknames like *Spacecase, Whirling*
   Dervish, or *Interplanet Janet*
3. Your own and your family's history of ADHD, depression, substance abuse,
   anxiety

might reveal that therapy or medication is also warranted, and if you ignore that aspect of your struggles, you could sabotage even your best efforts at coaching yourself. (See medication table, page 232.)

But assuming that you're emotionally and physically able to act as your own coach—that you are ready, willing, and able to meet the challenge—let me give you an idea of what it will take.

The Little Black Book

One of my best teachers required that each of us in his class keep a journal, which most of us vehemently resisted at first but which we later came to appreciate. "It will help you remember who you were," he used to tell us, and as with most other things he said, he was right about the power of that notebook to capture the past. To this day, one look at its soft, familiar cover and frayed edges brings every teenage embarrassment painfully to life!

Now I want you to get a notebook of your own, not to spill onto its pages the yearnings of a restless heart, but to organize in a practical way those goals you hope to attain and the strategies you'll devise to get you there. As long as you can chart your progress and setbacks—as long as you can observe yourself along this self-coaching journey—any type of notebook or journal will be fine, but a three-ring binder has the advantage of letting you add pages and/or move them from one section to another.

You can begin the notebook by adapting a worksheet I ask my clients to complete when we begin our coaching process. And because no "right" or "wrong" answers to the questions exist, you should be as honest as possible in answering them. They're not meant as a judgment. They're meant as a guide, a way to get a picture of who you are and how you're living now, right at this moment. If you have trouble answering, try reading the questions out loud or taking a short break and coming back to them later. Don't overanalyze anything. Simply write what comes to mind.

COACHING GOALS AND ABILITIES
WORKSHEET

1. PROFESSIONAL LIFE

Am I in the job or profession for which my education prepared me? (Am I doing what I was trained to do?)

_____

If not, why?

_____

What does it mean to me to have—or have *not*—taken the path for which I prepared?

_____

What do I do *well* in my job?

_____

What specific parts of my job do I actually enjoy?

_____

What problems do I experience in my job?

_____

Would I choose this job again if I were starting over?

_____

How much of my job do I have to "bring home"?

_____

What words best describe how I feel when I think about my job?

_____

2. PHYSICAL HEALTH

How much sleep do I generally get?

_____

When I wake up, do I feel rested?

_____

Do I eat three meals a day regularly?

_____

Do I limit calories, fat, sodium, and the like in my food?

_____

Is my weight under control?

_____

What medications do I regularly take?

_____

Do I exercise on a regular basis?

_____

Do I limit my alcohol consumption?

_____

Have I stopped smoking? (Or have I never started?)

_____

Am I happy with the state of my present physical health?

_____

3. SOCIAL LIFE

How often do I see my friends?

_____

Do my friends and acquaintances "lift me up," or do they "drag me down"?

_____

How often do I have fun?

_____

What do I enjoy doing beyond work?

_____

4. SPIRITUAL LIFE AND SENSE OF WELL-BEING

How important to me is being part of a religious community like a church or synagogue?

_____

Is being _spiritual_, rather than _religious_, important to me?

_____

How often do I pray or meditate?

_____

When do I feel most at peace?

_____

What makes me feel a sense of gratitude?

_____

What makes me feel fulfilled?

_____

What stressors are present in my life?

_____

Who are the people in my support network?

_____

How often do I interact with those in my support network?

_____

What do I do for *myself only*?

_____

What do I value most in life?

_____

What do I do to honor those values?

_____

5. FINANCIAL CONSIDERATIONS

How often do I worry about money?

_____

Have I saved enough for emergencies?

_____

Do I have long-term investments?

_____

Do I have adequate health/home/life insurance?

_____

Am I living within my means?

_____

How do I generally regard the concept of debt?

_____

What do I consider important enough to incur debt for?

_____

How manageable is my current debt?

_____

How financially secure do I feel?

_____

6. HOME LIFE

What quality time am I spending with my spouse or partner?

_____

Is that time sufficient?

_____

What quality time am I spending with my children?

_____

Is it enough?

_____

How important are my individual needs to my family?

_____

How am I handling my share of family responsibilities?

_____

How do I feel about the area where I live?

_____

How does my home reflect who I am?

_____

Read over the responses you gave to these questions. Take enough time to think about what you wrote. What profile of you emerges? With that picture in mind, it's time to answer a few more questions:

1. **IN WHICH AREAS OF MY LIFE DO I APPEAR MOST IN CONTROL?**

2. **IN WHICH AREAS DO I APPEAR MOST SATISFIED OR CONTENT?**

3. **IN WHICH AREAS DO I APPEAR TO BE STRUGGLING?**

4. **ARE THERE ANY AREAS WHERE I APPEAR UNFULFILLED?**

Before reading any further, think back to what I said earlier in the book about the importance of balance in a person's life. Coaching, I remind you, is holistic. It seeks to address all areas of a client's life and to guide the client toward balance.

Now it's time for you to answer several more questions, all based on what you have already indicated about the way you're living:

1. **WHAT ARE SOME KEY AREAS IN MY LIFE THAT I WANT TO IMPROVE?**

   (Health? Finances? Professional development? Home life? Social life? Spiritual life?)

2. **WHAT ARE SEVERAL OF MY SHORT-TERM GOALS?**

   Where do I want to be in one month?

   Three months?

   Six months?

   What do I have to do daily to get there?

   What things do I want to work on now?

3. **WHAT ARE MY LONG-TERM GOALS?**

4. **HOW DO MY GOALS REFLECT WHAT I SAY I VALUE MOST?**

   (Before answering, refer back to the section on spiritual life and sense of well-being, page 38.)

5. WHAT MUST I DO—WHAT CHANGES WILL I HAVE TO MAKE—IN ORDER TO LIVE ACCORDING TO MY VALUES?

Reading the information you provided and assessing the overall sense of how you're living might have surprised you, or it might have upset or disconcerted you. It's important to have thought about all these aspects of your life, though, because it will help you later as you construct a plan for acting as your own coach.

To facilitate your coaching, and especially to help you begin, you must keep your notebook in a safe, convenient place where you'll have ready access to it. It will become your constant reference through the process of self-coaching. It's where you'll write down your goals, note your progress and setbacks, and clarify your thinking. It's really the proof, the confirmation, of where you have been and where you are headed. It's the truth that stands up boldly to the self-delusion so many of us practice.

In its own way, the notebook that you keep can be the best accountability partner you'll ever know. If you're honest about what you put into it, it will be unrelenting in its honesty in return. "I feel like a schoolboy again, always carrying my notebook around," a client told me recently. "But I'd be lost without it. It's like my old friend Jack from high school, the one who kept me on the straight and narrow. My folks used to say that Jack was the one who kept me honest."

The notebook will also be demanding, especially of the attention it deserves. No matter how difficult the notion of writing in it might seem now, you'll need to commit to it if you're going to succeed, which means developing a new habit, or ritual, of record keeping. Make it easy on yourself by eliminating potential problems before they begin: Keep the notebook visible, keep it in the same place, keep a pen right next to it, set a specific time to update it, post reminders to yourself that it's waiting for you! Treat your notebook like a friend or trusted ally who wants only the best for you, and it will reward you in ways you can actually document.

On the other hand, in this era of technology, a notebook might not work for you. George, a former client, prefers electronic devices, so he uses his computer to record his goals and successes and setbacks, and he returns to his file daily. He also relies heavily on his PDA. "For me, the PDA is a godsend," he told me after we'd worked together for a while. "I can keep track of things, dates, times, phone numbers, account information, passwords—everything, really—better than my wife, the walking calendar. It's like an extension of my brain."

Each person has to develop the tools and strategies that work individually, so think about your own needs and tendencies, the most comfortable ways you know of keeping track of things. The important thing is that you own the system you create or you won't stick with it. As George put it, "Whatever ways fit your individual style, you need to maintain them like they're a life-support system."

Choose what works for you and stick to it. Just promise yourself to *use* your notebook or your computer file or whatever other electronic device you decide on. The goal is to keep track of what you want to accomplish, whatever way you choose to do that.

How to Self-Coach

Just as *partnership*, *structure*, and *process* are the core elements of my coaching model, they will be the fundamentals of your self-coaching. And the goal will be developing the ability to self-initiate change.

PARTNERSHIP

Self-coaching requires that you learn as much as you can about your own neurobiology. You need to partner with your brain to exploit your strengths and overcome your weaknesses. Essentially, you need to take control and acknowledge—truly understand— that your ADHD brain is part of who you are and that you *can control* that part.

But you should also create outside accountability partners, trusted advisers with whom you can touch base and who are willing and able to commit to you. Again, because it's usually easier for others to see us than it is to see ourselves, it's important to select people who will be nonjudgmental as well as objective. These partnerships will help guide and direct you when you get off course.

STRUCTURE

I know that structure is inherently difficult for people with ADHD, but to self-coach on this journey, you must put boundaries, or structures, in place for your ADHD brain to follow. That's a central paradox in the concept of coaching. The very structure that an ADHD brain resists is the actual means to harnessing that brain, to making it work *for* you. As one of my clients put it, "Coaching is very structured, which is hard for me, but that's why I requested help in the first place—my lack of structure!"

But once again, you have to be honest about building those essential structures, even as you resist the urge to abandon them when you think they've become too challenging. If you keep your commitment to effect a change in your life, structures will help you develop the new habits that eventually become your instinctive ways to cope.

PROCESS

Change takes time. It also involves setbacks, but in the coaching process, there's a good reason why. The individualized approach that fosters individual success means that generic structures and strategies won't work. Much of the time, you'll be engaged in trial and error as you try to determine which approaches will be effective, but trial and error is part of what you should expect as you discover the strategies that work in your particular life.

Be aware that to succeed, you'll need to keep up a constant dialogue with yourself as you build and then modify or possibly eliminate strategies that aren't working. That's where your notebook or computer file can help. If you find yourself not following through on one of your strategies, for example, slow yourself down and list the actions you actually took instead of the actions detailed in your strategy.

Use your notes to question yourself the way I questioned David when he wasn't paying his bills once a week as he had planned. Your answer to "What did I do instead?" might reveal that you need to change your strategy and devise a plan that will work with your strengths and interests, not against them.

That kind of objective awareness—an actual written record—of what is holding you back, rather than a mere feeling of helplessness, is exactly what can help you take control of your actions and effect the changes you desire. It's worth noting that the notebook or file will also reflect your progress and the strategies that have been working, which can remind you, when necessary, to hold resolutely to your goals.

Understanding from the outset that coaching is a journey—that it's a process, the antithesis of instant gratification—can help you adhere to your commitment to take control of your life, even during those inevitable moments of frustration when you're tempted to turn away. Nobody will deny that it's easy to get down on yourself when you aren't making the progress you've envisioned. It's understandable, especially initially, to revert to the old ways of thinking and want to "pack it in and accept that you're a loser," as one of my clients said recently. But remember that you must separate the action from the person performing the action so you can move past blame and discouragement and into positive action. Coaching works when it has been given the time to work, so promise yourself to stay with it!

DECISION TIME

Consider the following questions to determine if you're ready to try self-coaching:

- Am I willing to let go of old patterns and habits in order to replace them with new ones?
- Am I able to identify at least one or two things I would like to change?
- Am I flexible enough to try new approaches to old ways of doing things?
- Am I willing to put the time and energy into the self-coaching process to get the results I want?
- Am I willing to be honest with myself in terms of what my effort level really is, rather than what I wish it would be at any given point?
- Do I have the courage to ask help from others?

The more times you answered *"yes"* to these questions, the more ready you are to try self-coaching. But there's a good chance you now have a question of your own, the same question almost every client asks: "How do I do it?"

Fortunately, I've devised a way to answer that question, which you'll discover when you turn to chapter 4. First, though, let's review what you can gain.

THE BENEFITS OF COACHING

1. Identifying your specific strengths and weaknesses
2. Setting realistic goals
3. Learning to prioritize
4. Creating necessary structures so you can stay on track to meet deadlines

5. Using strategies without giving up; becoming more resilient
6. Improving organizational and time management skills
7. Self-motivating by means of your "internal dialogue" and self-observation
8. Learning productive ways in which to handle the details of your daily life
9. Improving personal habits, such as exercise and nutrition
10. Developing an assertive outlook to advocate and get the support you need
11. Communicating more effectively with those around you
12. Setting up a more efficient environment to meet your needs

Can you do it? You won't know until you try, so I urge you to make the effort. It won't necessarily be easy, and I can't guarantee you'll succeed, but I *can* guarantee that if you make a serious effort, you'll learn something about how your ADHD brain operates. You'll also learn much more about yourself as an individual,

COACHING AND THERAPY
(See Appendix B for ways to locate an ADHD coach.)
by John J. Ratey, M.D.

Whether you decide to work with an ADHD coach or self-coach, it should be clear from the start that coaching is not a substitute for therapy or any other services that may be beneficial to you. In fact, the collaborative efforts of coaching and therapy can often produce the best results. It should also be very clear that coaching or self-coaching is not a substitute for medication. The combination of medication prescribed by a physician familiar with ADHD, along with therapy and coaching, or self-coaching, can serve as a multifaceted approach to improving the quality of life for someone with ADHD.

about who you are and how you are living, about the goals you're willing to strive for and the compromises you're willing, and unwilling, to make.

And with the power that this new knowledge brings, you can absolutely change the way you live into living in a way you love. You might even repeat what Gary, a former client, told me not too long ago: "I am who I am today because of it. Coaching literally changed my life."

Now it's *your* turn to turn around *your* life. You really are the only person who can change it, but let me help you begin. Let me give you the answer!

CHAPTER 4

Finding the A-N-S-W-E-R

To help you make the changes you want, I've developed a strategic tool I call the **A-N-S-W-E-R**.

The **A-N-S-W-E-R** is the practical guide to coaching yourself. It helps you move past the shame and incompetence your ADHD often makes you feel and into the self-understanding and acceptance that everyone needs in order to live a full life. By following its process, you can effectively begin to take control of your challenges, using strength-based strategies that you devise yourself to address them.

As you already know, wishing and hoping will never be enough to change you or get you where you want to be. If you truly want to make a change in your life, you have to do something—two things, really: First you need to make a plan, and then you need to make an effort to follow that plan.

But don't just forge ahead blindly, as you might be tempted to do. Instead, as you consider a plan to change your life into one that fulfills you, one that you actually love living, I want you to be guided by those principles and ideas that you yourself listed on your **Coaching Goals and Abilities Worksheet** (see page 36).

Look back at number 4, "Spiritual Life and Sense of Well-Being." You listed there what you value most in life and what you currently do to honor those values. A little later you stated what you have to change in order to live a life based on those values.

Before you read any further, turn to a clean page in your notebook or computer file and title it **"Mission Statement,"** which is a promise to yourself that every change you attempt to make will be shaped by those principles or ideals that you hold inviolate, those values that you are no longer willing to compromise. Remember: If you are going to live a life that reflects what you hold sacred—a life that reflects your core values—you need to know what that actually means. If you can't put it into words, then you might not have thought about it enough. Take the time to think right now, and when you are ready, write it clearly and unequivocally under the **"Mission Statement"** heading on your page.

To help you begin thinking about your own, let me give you two examples. One client had been growing increasingly frustrated by the many demands on his time and energy that were leaving him unfulfilled. He felt physically exhausted, he said, and emotionally depleted, but he was beginning to understand that he could not keep meeting everyone else's needs if he did not also meet at least a few of his own. He wrote as his mission statement, "I will take care of my mind, body, and spirit, so that I have the strength to take care of my family's needs." He would base future decisions, he said, on how well they would honor that statement.

Another client was feeling guilty about her inability to be the same model of perfection socially as she was professionally, and she frequently found herself angry and short-tempered with friends and acquaintances, who she believed were expecting too much of her. They, in turn, found her inconsiderate and aloof when she turned down invitations and didn't check in with them as often as they expected. In her mission statement, she resolved, "I will live a more fulfilling life where I am more accepting and forgiving of myself and others, and where I am also honest with myself and others."

People with ADHD can be more directed when they have a clear vision of what they want to accomplish, so craft a powerful mission statement that will help you adhere to your most important values.

Your mission statement needs to be anchored in your brain, and you can best anchor it by verbalizing it. That's why you need to articulate it. That's why you need to write it down. But don't just walk away from it once you do. Review it daily. Say it out loud. Make it your mantra. Engineer your environment so that you see it easily. In addition to writing it in your notebook, stick it on your bulletin board or affix it to your mirror. Create a screen saver with it. Do whatever you must to keep that mission statement at the forefront of your mind. Knowing and repeating what you truly value will help you in every change you attempt to make.

How the A-N-S-W-E-R Works

Each of you reading this book is at a particular place in your life, so each of you is at a slightly different point along the continuum of change. You might, for example, be further along than others in acknowledging that you really do have ADHD struggles. You might be well aware of your challenges but not actively developing strategies to overcome them. Or you might have been working hard but employing the wrong strategies for your specific personalities or circumstances.

Ultimately, each of you has to design an individual plan to overcome your individual challenges. The word *ANSWER* is an acronym for the six basic steps you'll need to follow as you begin to coach yourself into control of your life.

1. **A**cknowledge and accept your ADHD and associated challenges.

2. **N**arrow in on one or two issues on which you initially want to work.

3. **S**trategize a plan of attack using strength-based structures.

4. **W**ork and follow the plan.

5. **E**valuate your progress on a regular basis to see what is working and what is not.

6. **R**epeat the process so your guard does not let down.

You will use and customize the **A-N-S-W-E-R** to suit your own needs.

A. ACKNOWLEDGE AND ACCEPT YOUR ADHD

Since the first step to solving a problem is acknowledging that the problem exists, you must acknowledge that you have ADHD, which means the following:

1. Recognizing that ADHD is part of your daily life

2. Understanding that it will not just go away

3. Learning as much as you can about your particular deficits

4. Admitting that many of the struggles and problems you experience are because of ADHD

Acknowledging your ADHD is meant as neither a crutch nor an excuse. It is simply an acceptance that ADHD is a fact of your life, one you can, and must, address. As one of my clients put it in his initial coaching session, "If you concentrate on what is *not* working in your life, you get stuck. You become a victim of this or that. I'm ready to move on from that. I've realized that my ADHD will never go away. It will always be with me. It's a matter of how I choose to deal with it. It's a choice. I want to learn how to live life not as a victim."

My client was right. Although you certainly have no choice about the existence of your ADHD, you absolutely do have a choice in what you can do about it. Step one is acknowledging its role in your life as a condition you can address.

But in order to address your ADHD, you must first understand it. Only then can you take the second important step in compensating for your ADHD symptoms: creating an emotional distance between who you are as a person and what you are doing because of your ADHD. As I've said before, you must learn to separate the action from the person performing the action.

How much do you understand about ADHD? Do you know how and why your ADHD affects the various areas of your life? Can you give examples of your ADHD challenges? A critical self-evaluation is an essential first step in self-coaching.

Self-Evaluation

Using your notebook or computer file, label a clean page "**Self-Evaluation**" and then make three columns on that page. Now write "**Symptom**" at the top of the left column and "**Outcome**" at the top of the right column. Leave the middle column blank, and we'll fill it in later. The page should look like this:

SELF-EVALUATION

SYMPTOM   OUTCOME

To begin, list under "**Symptom**" one behavior or symptom of your ADHD, and directly across from that, under "**Outcome**," name *all* the effects that particular symptom has on your life, trying to be as specific as possible. Then keep going, listing all symptoms and all effects in the same manner. Take as long as you need, using as many pages as you need, keeping in mind that in order to change your life, which is your general goal, you have to be honest about the changes you need to make, which are your specific goals.

To help you get started, consider symptoms and outcomes that many of my clients have listed in their own notebooks:

SELF-EVALUATION

SYMPTOM	OUTCOME
Poor sense of time	Always late
	Accomplishes little
	Seen as undependable
Difficulty prioritizing	Often disappoints others
	Does work on wrong projects
	Avoids important tasks
Acting before thinking; getting bored easily	Spotty employment history
	Can't maintain relationships
	Can't tolerate boredom
Easily sidetracked from goal	Jumps from task to task
	Doesn't listen to others
	Misses deadlines
Inflexible; stuck in details	Can't let go
	Too controlling
	Easily agitated

Now chart your own symptoms and their impact on both you and those close to you.

If you have difficulty, or if you aren't sure of either your negative behavior patterns or their effect on others, you might consider asking someone else to look over your list. Sometimes objective observers have a way of seeing us that we never have ourselves, and sometimes we aren't aware of how our actions are affecting other people. Making this list is the perfect time to ask the assistance of an accountability partner. You want to begin your self-coaching journey in as honest and open a way as possible, after all, so if someone can help you take this first step, by all means try it.

But I must stress again what I have already said to you several times in this book and what I find myself repeating over and over to my clients: *Adults with ADHD are usually masters in the art of self-deception.* Accountability, to yourself or others, works only in proportion to your individual honesty about your ADHD. Consider what one former client revealed early on in our coaching journey. "I got so good at hiding my inferiorities around others that I can easily fool myself," he said. "Even during years of football playing—and I was a high school all-star—no one could tell that I hardly knew what a 'down' was, let alone what down it was at any given point in the game. I'm so good at deception—hiding or sneaking candy, bad grades, cigarettes—that I have mastered self-accountability deception."

If you're going to serve as your own coach, you absolutely cannot deceive yourself about your ADHD. You must be honest about how your ADHD affects your life by taking the time to learn how your ADHD brain operates. Once you understand the characteristics of ADHD, you should see that ADHD is controlling much of your behavior. This ability to step back and separate the person from the problem—this new objectivity about your behavior—will help you move past self-blame and toward the changes you've promised yourself you'll make.

Acknowledging your ADHD, then, means more than simply stating that you have it. It means examining how you are acting because of ADHD and how your actions are affecting others. It means consistently reminding yourself that ADHD is a problem requiring your steady, unrelenting determination to address its symptoms.

IN THE A-N-S-W-E-R, *ACKNOWLEDGMENT* MEANS:

• Understanding that you have ADHD

• Learning what that means in general terms

• Actively examining what it means in your own life

• Separating your ADHD from yourself (I *have* ADHD, not I *am* ADHD)

• Moving past self-blame

• Taking responsibility for yourself

• Taking action to change your behavior patterns

• Creating accountability with others, if necessary

N. NARROW THE FOCUS

"Looking at my goals, I can see that they're all over the map," a client told me recently. "I need to edit and consolidate. I know my heart's desire but don't know how to make it happen. Where do I begin?"

Because most ADHD adults voice the same frustration about their own goals and challenges, you can probably relate to my client's plea for help. But once you have separated yourself from your ADHD—once you acknowledge that *ADHD is a condition, it's not who I am*—you should be able to identify the key challenges it presents, focusing on two or three major issues with which you most frequently struggle.

You can *narrow the focus* by referring back to the symptoms and outcomes you listed in acknowledging your ADHD (see pages 53–54). Directly beneath your list, write and complete the following statement:

THE AREAS THAT CAUSE ME THE MOST DIFFICULTY ARE

• _____

• _____

• _____

In your enthusiasm to get started, you probably want to make a change for every symptom you've listed, but it's essential that you initially address only one or two issues, preferably one. Earlier, you listed several short-term goals that you wanted to work on. Go back and compare what you wrote then with the symptoms and outcomes you listed later. Can you select from the lists one or two common symptoms with which to begin self-coaching? Draw a circle around those symptoms, and complete the following statements on a clean page:

MY FIRST GOAL IS TO ADDRESS THE FOLLOWING SYMPTOMS OR BEHAVIORS:

_____

_____

Then complete the following statement:

I HOPE TO CHANGE THE FOLLOWING SPECIFIC OUTCOMES:

_____

_____

If this seems like a modest beginning to your coaching journey, and that selecting only one or two challenges rather than all the behaviors keeping you from the balanced life I said was so important is a small goal, it's for a good reason.

I want you to succeed at self-coaching. I don't want you to set up a losing proposition by trying to change too many things at once. Do you remember what I said earlier about running? Just as I wouldn't allow a novice to attempt a marathon on the first day out, neither would I allow a new client to work on multiple challenges at once, especially before fully understanding the ADHD causes behind his or her actions. In either case, the likely outcome would be failure and disappointment, possibly even refusal to try again. The client, like the runner, would be overwhelmed by the enormity of the task. Who would blame either one of them for thinking, "Never again!"

Unfortunately, I'm all too familiar with clients who set themselves up for failure. "This is my last chance," they often think. "If I don't change everything at once, it's not worth it." Even if they succeed at narrowing their goals, they might lack an understanding of what each goal will take—the amount of time, for instance, or the effort involved to accomplish it. They become so easily frustrated by effort and long-term commitment that they give up before they give themselves a chance to succeed. My job as coach is to remind them of narrowing the focus. As your own coach, you have to remind yourself.

The point is to master one goal at a time so you can explore associated patterns and behaviors that normally prevent you from attaining your goals. In this way, you can employ countermeasures against those obstacles. My job as coach is to keep one goal at a time in the forefront of my client's mind. That must be your goal, too.

If you give yourself permission to proceed slowly and deliberately, you'll realize another benefit. Instead of simply changing specific outcomes of your ADHD symptoms, you'll understand their causes as well. This knowledge is important because once you identify patterns of behavior, you can also identify triggers that lead you off course. To succeed at self-coaching, knowing what takes you off course is essential.

One of the most common deterrents for adults with ADHD in reaching their goals is their inner saboteur—the negative tapes inside the head that constantly remind them of past failures. But once you understand that the actions you want to change occur because of your ADHD brain—again, once you understand that you, the person, are separate from your actions—you can eliminate the blame and embarrassment and discouragement you've suffered for years. Every time you focus on what draws you away from your goal, you can then implement a strategy to eliminate that obstacle, rather than repeating the negative tape that tells you you're incompetent or irresponsible or hopeless. You can actually develop those new habits and actions we have already agreed are essential to success.

Remember, you don't have to be a victim at the mercy of an omnipotent force. You can choose to *act* against it.

In the **A-N-S-W-E-R,** *Narrowing the Focus* means:
- Zeroing in on the negative aspects of the specific behaviors
- Navigating the traps and distractions you repeatedly face
- Selecting the one or two challenges most negatively affecting your life
- Eliminating the negative tapes that can sabotage your efforts

One of my clients really enjoys the view from her creekfront deck. "I love to look at the houses across the water and watch the people working on their boats or in their gardens," she told me not too long ago. "I can see each one distinctly. I wish I could look at my goals that way—individually and distinctly. With goals and challenges and my ADHD behaviors, I feel like I'm looking at an ocean with no end in sight, not a creek that gives me a view of the other side. I'm overwhelmed by the vastness of what's in front of me."

When she said that, I told her the same thing my father told me when I asked him one day how he always managed to stay focused when he obviously had to contend with so many obligations to so many people in so many different aspects of his life. He thought for a moment before reminding me of the camera he'd recently bought for my mother, the one with the zoom lens.

"Suppose you want to take a picture of the backyard here," he said, "but you can't get everything into one shot. Instead, you decide to feature the apple tree in the corner, but even that tree is really too big, so now you zoom in on a single branch, but even that isn't quite small enough, so you finally choose one leaf, or one apple, and you zoom in really close and take that particular picture. That's what I do when I have so many things to think about. I zoom in. I narrow my focus."

So there it is, another part of the **A-N-S-W-E-R**. In my father's honor, I encourage you to narrow the focus. Doing so will allow you to navigate the traps and eliminate the negative tapes and consequences you have endured for far too long.

S. STRATEGIZE! STRATEGIZE AGAIN!

As I learned even before my official diagnosis of ADHD, I had to find ways to compensate for the particular deficits that threatened to hold me back. When I lived at home, my father took the lead for me. But once I left home, I had to learn for myself how to *strategize*—how to create a specific plan to address my specific ADHD challenges.

Now you must do the same. Frankly, it doesn't matter if your husband organizes his clothing according to color or your wife exercises each morning exactly two hours after coffee and the news. If that works for them, then let them enjoy the rewards of what they've structured, but don't get caught in the trap of assuming that their routines should be yours.

Unfortunate as it may initially appear, there are no prepackaged strategies for success as you address your ADHD challenges. It might be easy and it might be convenient if it were otherwise, but the simple truth is this: Other people's routines can be useless or even counterproductive for you, so you have to commit to the process of creating your own. Fortunately, there's an upside. Not only do you get to be creative, you also get to acknowledge and work to your strengths along the way.

As I discovered during my graduate school days at Harvard, your strategies don't have to be driven by "I *should*." Don't let that kind of thinking—"I *should* do such and such because everybody else does"—set you up for failure the way it did me.

Finding Your Own Strategies

An assignment was due, and I was well aware that if I didn't sit down and focus, I would never finish the work. I was desperate, but I was proud, too. At last I had come up with a plan to keep myself seated and finally complete the paper I had been writing— or not writing—for more than a month. After spreading my books across the library table where I had settled, I sat for a moment and smiled, confident at being part of the serious population in this dark-paneled room I had so often avoided. Today would be different, I knew. Then today would turn to night, and still I would sit, still I would stay, still I would be in this seat when the lights at last dimmed. Smiling at the perfection of my plan, I removed the sweatshirt I had been wearing for the occasion and, using its arms as a rope, carefully tied my own leg to the leg of the mahogany table in front of me, secure in the knowledge that I would not be wandering off. I would sit as long as it took, and I would finish my work.

Much to my dismay, the only reward for my trouble was that I fell asleep.

And when I woke, it was not to the perfectly penned paper I had hoped to produce, but to panic at what I was sure was imminent failure.

Yet what a liberating lesson I learned in the Harvard library that day! I discovered the fallacy in my thinking, the assumption that my experience disproved. I assumed that if I did what everybody else was doing, I would get the same results. I assumed that since all the other students sat at a table in the library, I should sit there, too. I assumed that if they did their work sitting still for hours, that's how I should do my work; if that's how they got their A's, that's how I should get my A's. I should sit still at a table in the library, and I would complete my assignment.

But I had overlooked a major factor in the equation: I simply was not someone who could sit still for long periods anywhere, much less in a silent library. Once I admitted that to myself, I realized that my apartment was actually a much better place for me to be. There, I could stand up or walk around without bothering people; I could take a break and then return to my work with better focus and resolve. And I discovered a built-in bonus as well: My apartment could become spotless in the process. Homework could be interspersed with housework, making neither the endless and oppressive drudgery it had usually been.

What a liberating lesson, indeed, one I happily pass on to you now: *There is no "one size fits all" approach to strategies for persons with ADHD.* You do not bear the burden of assuming others' routines for yourself. Do what works for you. Your brain is unique, so the way to accommodate yourself will also be unique.

That's the point. It's up to you to discover strategies that work for you.

Doing What Works for You

Katherine, one of my former clients, had left her position as a designer in a large firm to work independently from an office in the fixer-upper she and her husband had recently purchased. Driven by the happy labor of renovating and decorating this dream-come-true cottage in the woods, Katherine soon faced the improbable prospect of losing that dream when her salary slipped considerably. Coaching helped her to realize that instead of concentrating on work for which she would be compensated, she had been spending an inordinate amount of time painting and wallpapering her new home. Once she understood how her priorities had shifted to another extreme—all work, no play had turned into all play, no work—she made a contract with herself. Recognizing the need for pursuing her avocation as well as her vocation, she decided to devote one hour to her own redecorating only after devoting four hours to work projects.

The reward system worked. Katherine was soon earning the salary she needed, and she still got to do what she loved. She used the decorating as her "reward" and let that be the motivation to do her "real" job. After all, if she didn't make the necessary money, she couldn't keep paying for the house and the countless ways in which it would finally become her own.

Another client, Steven, was a caseworker who had been struggling to track his various cases. "I need to *see* all the cases," he told me. "I have to lay everything out—their specifics, their relative importance, their time frames—in the context of a full month. Otherwise, they get all mixed up in my head and I can't remember which ones I should be working on at any given time."

After exploring several options, Steven decided that what he really needed was a wall-size calendar, but because he worked in an open office setting, he had been too embarrassed to address his tracking problem "publicly." After a few sessions of my relentless prodding, he decided to purchase a whiteboard with a monthly calendar; he assigned each case a particular color and then began tracking them on the calendar with Post-it notes to match. Interestingly, the standing and moving required to physically track the cases this way helped to stimulate his brain, which in turn kept him more alert and less inclined to become confused. The benefits were so immediate and so strong that, much to Steven's surprise, wall calendars soon became part of the office decor.

Seeing Your Strengths

Unlikely as it might seem, successful strategizing involves more than acknowledging your weaknesses or deficits. It involves acknowledging your strengths as well, which sounds like another paradox to many of my clients.

Accustomed to the negative tapes testifying to their incompetence, adults with ADHD are often blind to their own talents and gifts and unaware of how much they've actually accomplished. One former client, an academic chairperson at a prestigious university, was plagued by feelings of failure. Despite her long career in both teaching and publishing, when I asked her to list her strengths, she could think of little in her life of which she could be proud. "I still remember," she told me, "how I couldn't complete one of my high school assignments. The class was called Teenage Problems, and the teacher made us list all the things we liked about ourselves and then all the things we didn't like. I could only do the last list. I left the whole first column blank."

Too many adults with ADHD are so focused on what they can't do that they forget the positive aspects of who they are and what they've managed to achieve, their ADHD deficits notwithstanding. They think that if something comes easily to them, there's only one of two reasons why: Either they're doing it incorrectly, or it must come easily to everyone else, too. Having spent their whole lives listening to criticism, they don't even have language for their own success. Many have practiced for so long covering up their weaknesses that they simply cannot acknowledge that they do anything well.

You have to change that thinking if you're going to create successful strategies for your ADHD challenges, so let's begin right now with a few questions I ask my clients in our initial sessions.

Before you answer, look back at your **Coaching Goals and Abilities Worksheet** (page 36), which is a reflection of balance in addressing the multiple layers of your life. In each section are opportunities for you to consider ways in which you are functioning well. Under "Professional Life," for example, if you're in the job for which you were educated, then perhaps that's something for which you should take credit. Once upon a time you chose to attend law school, for example, and now you're an associate at a large firm near your home. Or once upon a time you chose to earn a master's degree in business, and now you head a company with markets overseas. In other words, you fulfilled a long-term goal, so might that also indicate something positive about your ability to prioritize or to see a plan through to completion? Under "Physical Health," perhaps you noted that, yes, you exercise regularly, and no, you no longer smoke. Might those choices speak to your iron will or your ability to focus on the goal?

Now read through the worksheet carefully, as if the person it represents were not you, but a job applicant for a position you're trying to fill. Let the worksheet represent a stranger, someone you've never met. As you read, underline every answer that indicates an asset or a measure of success. Then complete the following statement:

I CAN SEE THAT "THE APPLICANT" HAS BEEN SUCCESSFUL AT:

- _____

- _____

- _____

- _____

- _____

You probably perceive the "anonymous" person on the worksheet as someone with more than a few positive qualities and accomplishments. I know that it's difficult to see yourself that way, but try to be objective. Read through the worksheet again, taking time to think about how your answers reflect your strengths. Then turn to a clean page in your notebook or computer file and answer the following questions. Again, try to answer truthfully, not according to "I should."

STRATEGIES WORKSHEET

What are my strengths?

What seems to come naturally to me?

I enjoy doing _____ (fill in blank) most in life.

What special skills or attributes do people notice about me?

What kinds of positive feedback do I receive from others?

What kinds of cues do I respond to? Visual? Auditory?

Recognizing Your Own Cues

When I ask my clients about cues, most of them don't know how to respond, so I usually follow up with a few other questions. I might ask, for example, "Do you post notes to yourself?" "Does making lists help you?" If they answer "yes," I tell them that they most likely respond to visual cues. But if they get overwhelmed by Post-it notes and prefer alarms sounding on their PDA, computer, or wristwatch, they most likely respond to auditory cues.

Brian, for example, frequently misplaces things, which is generally not a problem, he said, because he can find them easily, too. To help him determine the types of cues that would work best for him in other circumstances, I asked him to take me through the process of locating his missing keys. "I have sort of a photographic memory," he said. "It's like there's a videocamera constantly running in my mind, so I can sort of *see* where they probably are."

After we discussed the way he retrieves missing items by use of his "X-ray vision," Brian realized that he responded to visual cues, information he could then use to create appropriate structures to meet his ADHD challenges. You can do the same by thinking about areas in which you typically do well and then basing the structures you build on either auditory cues—setting alarms and beepers, for example—or visual cues—posting notes and reminders to yourself.

Borrowing What Works

Successful strategizing definitely requires effort. Sometimes that means thinking about what is working in one aspect of your life but is absent from another. If you seem to be leading a double life, what structures are in place in one area that are missing in the other?

"I'm so incompetent," Caroline, a stay-at-home mom and chairwoman of the Cultural Arts Committee for her large suburban school district, told me in an early coaching session.

Frustrated by her inability to keep a warm and welcoming home that was also neat and organized, and feeling like a failure at "no-brainer nonsense like a clean kitchen," Caroline never considered the years of diverse and expanding programs she had overseen in her volunteer position in the PTA. Asked to explain how she operated in that capacity, she said, "Oh, that's easy. I can really 'see the forest,' so I know what programs I want to bring in, and I can 'see the trees,' too. I absolutely see how I want the year to evolve and what each program should include. And then I delegate—I put other people in charge of carrying out the details along the way. If I had to take care of the details myself, forget it. I'd get bogged down and then nothing would ever happen."

Caroline understood that although she could also see the forest and the trees at home, she could never quite carry out the plan to make her goals real. Through coaching, she realized that to accomplish her goal—the lived-in, nonchaotic refuge she believed her family deserved—she could borrow from her success in district projects by applying the same principle at home: She could delegate.

"I wonder why I never just hired somebody in the first place," Caroline said several months into the new routine of a weekly housekeeper. Giving herself permission to seek outside help had not been easy, but once she saw the benefit—her home was at last the inviting sanctuary she had envisioned—Caroline felt liberated from the self-imposed burden of perfection she had too long carried. The dizzying praise she'd always heard for her committee work had been addictive. Needing to feel the same pride elsewhere— indeed, everywhere—in her life, she had been unable to admit the limitations precluding it. Instead, she had spent years trying to deny the most universal human quality we know: fallibility.

Sadly, I didn't have to think too hard about why Caroline had resisted help. In the same way that adults with ADHD feel as incompetent and unworthy as others have implied or stated for

years, they also exert great energy trying to hide their weaknesses.
To them, seeking help is equivalent to admitting failure. Perhaps
it's just another of the many paradoxes inherent in ADHD behavior, but the idea of simply stating, "I can't do this. Can you help?"
is abhorrent. It confirms every negative tape in their already self-
accusing heads.

What Caroline needed to understand is that she could—in fact,
she must—acknowledge her weaknesses and address them in the
best ways possible. Only after she slowed down and analyzed the issue without her negative tapes playing—only after she saw the situation strategically—was she finally able to come up with a tactic to
address it. Understanding at last that she didn't have to be
perfect—that there was no shame in admitting she couldn't do
everything well—she could take advantage of reliable outside help.

Caroline could also base her strategy on the same strength that
had served her in her cultural arts work. Always quick to assess
what needed to be done, she was equally perceptive assessing
which person should do it. Caroline understood well what another
client, a financial executive, had stated years ago. "You have to carefully choose the right level of expertise around you," he said, "so you
can learn to successfully delegate and not be in a position where
you're always teaching. That's the point of delegating, isn't it? To let
somebody else who knows how and what to do take charge."

As you self-coach, you can, and must, slow down enough to
see your issues strategically. Remember, coaching focuses on the
practical; it is outcome-based and goal-oriented. Concentrate
not on *why* you are doing something, but on *what* and *how*. Practice asking yourself the kinds of nonjudgmental questions I ask
my clients:

- What is the issue?
- What can I do about it?
- What strategies that are effective "there" can I also use "here"?

- How can I maintain progress?
- How can I set up accountability?

IN THE A-N-S-W-E-R, *STRATEGIZING* MEANS:
- Creating a plan for self-improvement
- Acknowledging your strengths as well as your challenges
- Matching strength-based strategies to those ADHD challenges
- Recognizing strategies and structures in one part of your life that you might implement in another
- Understanding the cues to which you respond
- Engineering your environment to meet your specific needs

Later in the book, I'll detail specific strength-based strategies my clients have created for addressing their specific ADHD issues. Then you can look back at the worksheets you've completed so far and develop strategies for your own challenges, tailored to your own strengths.

W. WORKING THE PLAN

"Why would I want to share a room with someone swinging from a chandelier?" Madeline, an artist living in Boulder, Colorado, asked the other day. We had been talking about the necessity of follow-through and commitment when Madeline offered her analogy to roommates. "It's like I'm sharing a room with myself," she said. "If I don't make a plan for the day, and if I don't have a strong sense of purpose in keeping the plan, I swear it's like living with a madwoman."

Keeping the plan, what I've termed *working the plan,* is definitely a challenging aspect of the **A-N-S-W-E-R** for most clients. But considering the culture in which we live, how could it be otherwise? Quick picks, instant access, instant abs: They're all there for the grabbing, society's push-of-the-button promises and results, effortless and easy and fingertip close.

Working the plan is anything but easy.

But working the plan is necessary.

And yes, working the plan requires effort—consistent effort, long effort, deep effort. But if you commit to the process of change—if you understand that change takes time—it will be rewarding effort as well.

Interestingly, most of my clients understand the importance of the long view. They state their goal, they know what they want, they develop their plan, and for the most part, they do so with enthusiasm, but the very enthusiasm that can spark effort often stems from an impulsivity that can lead them astray. "For years I've known I have to lose weight," said Amy, a Boston commercial real estate broker, "and a million times I've researched different diets or different gyms in my area. I sign on to a diet program or I find a gym I can go to before work, and no matter what I choose, something else winds up looking better, so I switch. I always get really excited about the idea in the beginning, and then—poof! A few weeks later, it's over. I can't tell you how many times I've done stuff like that. I never get anywhere."

Amy was hardly alone in being consistently inconsistent. Distracted by any number of other issues or ideas, adults with ADHD get sidetracked from the original goal and abandon their original plan before they've invested any time in carrying it out. Lack of consistency inevitably negates any progress they might have made and prevents the long-term benefits of the systems they've set up.

But if you're going to succeed—if you're going to reach the goals that you've chosen—you have to recognize the difference between making the plan and working the plan. Working it means sticking with it. It means fighting through both the obstacles that stand in the way and the frustration that delayed payback for immediate effort provokes. It means desire and then more desire and the refusal to give up.

Marvin, a hedge fund manager I coach, was echoing many of my clients when he lamented his struggles at the office. "It would sound crazy to people I work with," he said, "but I have never felt successful there. I never feel any continuity. I want to get into a flow where I'll finally be free of obstructions. I just can't keep reverting back to the same old behaviors that throw me off track."

Engineering the Environment

As you self-coach, consider what will help you commit to your long-term plan. You can start by engineering your environment—setting up reminders, like those auditory or visual cues I discussed earlier. If you respond to visual cues, for example, create a screen saver to remind you daily of your ultimate goal. If you prefer auditory cues, set alarms to keep you on task, or record messages to yourself—reminders of what you want to accomplish—and listen to them in your car as you're driving to and from work. Make a habit of repeating your mission statement, the mantra you created to guide you along.

More important, be aware of the nature and biology of ADHD—forgetting the importance of the goal—and don't get caught in that trap. Plan ahead by observing what gets you off track. In your notebook or PDA file, make note of those times you get sidetracked and create strategies to address what is keeping you from your goal.

Through coaching, Amy came to realize that three or four weeks after she had started any exercise program, she would abandon it for something new. Forewarned is forearmed, as my father used to say, so, using this insight, she created a strategy to address her old habit of cut and run. As she began her membership in yet another gym, she wrote and addressed a letter to herself, instructing her closest friend to mail it three weeks from that day. "Dear Amy," the letter said. "You've been going to the gym for three weeks and you're probably thinking about quitting again, but remember that **YOU WANT TO LOSE 20 POUNDS!!! KEEP GOING!!! DON'T QUIT!!! HANG IN THERE!!!**" Her goal clearly spelled out on the page in front of her, Amy would not likely turn away from the commitment she was trying to keep.

Amy understood her own history, and she had learned to acknowledge her ADHD. Knowing that her tendency was to live in the moment, and admitting that she could easily talk herself out of going to the gym, she was able to narrow in on the one thing that took her off course, forgetting the importance of her commitment. Knowing and accepting this part of her ADHD behavior allowed her to take action: She created a strategy to jolt her memory three weeks into her exercise program. By writing a letter beforehand, Amy reminded herself of her weak spot, which in turn helped her keep to her commitment.

Being Accountable

Amy also enlisted the service of a friend, a tactic that sometimes makes the difference between continuing and giving up. One of the lessons clients learn in coaching is the importance of accountability. Somehow the notion of enlisting another's help or answering to another for what you have done—or not done—can be a strong motivator, a reason to move forward when it seems easier to turn aside. An accountability partner can also help silence the negative tapes that threaten you into surrender, strongly urging that you *can do* when your own voice is whispering, *I can't.*

In the end, as one of my clients noted, you have to be your own best friend. "I used to think I had to take care of everybody else," Josh told me during one of our last sessions, "so I had to learn to work hard for myself, for the changes that I wanted to make. I had to learn how to be flexible, to set up a plan that works with my ADHD." Then he added, with energy and pride, "And I did."

IN THE A-NS-W-E-R, *WORKING THE PLAN* MEANS:

- Taking action
- Actively following the strategies you created
- Using your environment to keep you on track
- Reminding yourself of past consequences
- Enlisting others to help with your plan
- Being accountable to yourself and others you've enlisted
- Being willing to put in the time it takes to change
- Having a sense of purpose

If you are going to succeed in changing your life, you cannot underestimate the importance of having a sense of purpose. As Madeline put it, "Having a very high sense of purpose is key to completing any plan I make. Now I know that I can't just 'jump in' to a plan. I have to do it purposefully and be centered about it. Otherwise, I'm simply making a recipe for disaster, stirring it up and then watching it burn."

Choose the recipe for success, instead. Work that plan! Be willing to invest the time! Really want it!

E. EVALUATE THE PLAN

"It's funny how clear things are becoming since we started this coaching," Andrew, another of my clients, said the other day. "I can see now that I've always had a remarkable unconscious repertoire of behaviors to accommodate for the problems in my personal and professional life. None of them have been particularly healthy, and most of them are downright self-defeating. Mainly, I had to make sure people held me in impossibly high regard but would fondly excuse me from any concrete expectations."

Then he added an observation so rich in insight that it can affect your self-coaching journey as well: "Only because I've slowed down enough to think about what I'd been doing—to reflect—can I see this. And I think taking the necessary time has been the real difference in making the changes I listed as my goals way back when we started. I know everything in life seems ridiculously fast paced, but I still wonder why so few people understand the concept of time when it comes to change."

What Andrew was referring to is the incontrovertible truth about changing your life. As you self-coach, you cannot judge a strategy's success or failure after one or two attempts at implementing it. You have to take time to let it work, and you have to take time to evaluate whether it's working. The symptoms of your ADHD and the goals you hope to accomplish might be vastly different from Andrew's, but the responsibility of evaluating your progress belongs to each of you.

Coaching, remember, is a process, and the changes you seek happen not instantly, but incrementally over time, sometimes a very long time. Because success requires commitment, and because the strategies you design are as individual as your individual needs, trial and error is an inherent, and time-dependent, part of the process. As you self-initiate change, you have to evaluate constantly whether the strategies and structures you've created serve your goals. If you're heading steadily toward where you eventually want to be, then your strategy is apparently a good one and you can continue to leave it in place. But if you're falling behind or slipping off course, you'll have to make a correction.

In the **A-N-S-W-E-R,** that's what evaluating means: judging or appraising the success of your plan and strategy, and acting, or reacting, accordingly.

Sometimes modifying a plan is easier said than done for individuals with ADHD, not because they can't think of another strategy, but because they haven't taken the time to analyze what is wrong, and right, with the original one. One of my clients, for example, knew how quickly she would become impatient when she didn't get immediate results. "I could feel myself getting in a panic or a frenzy," Mariana told me, "and I'd wind up just ditching the entire plan. I never knew how to look at individual parts of it, so I never really knew which parts might be working and which parts weren't. I'd get so frustrated that I'd just give up on everything."

Through coaching, Mariana understood the importance of acknowledging her history of impatience in order to counteract it. In her notebook, she began to track her progress with the plan on which she was currently working, addressing specific structures within it. By slowing down to analyze discrete elements of her plan, she could evaluate each separately and then make the necessary changes, rather than give up entirely on what might, with a few adjustments, have been workable and successful.

Because slowing down to evaluate is essential to your own success, turn to a clean page in your notebook or file, and under the heading **"Evaluate,"** write down the following questions to help you assess your progress:

> **What is working in my plan?** Try to identify specific progress using this strategy, such as specific actions you're now taking.
>
> **Why is it working?** If you can identify why it works, you can use the information in creating other strategies.
>
> **What measures or system can I use to track my progress?**
>
> **If something is not working, what about it isn't?** Can you isolate one thing that isn't?
>
> **What can I do about it?** Remember David, who had selected the wrong day to pay his bills? A simple change like the one he made could make all the difference for you, too!
>
> **When will I do it?** A goal must have a specific start date, or it is merely a wish. Set a date to begin!
>
> **What is my commitment level?** On a scale of **1,** lowest, to **5,** highest, rank your commitment. Remember that it has to be **high** if you're going to succeed!

How can I remember my commitment to my goal? How can you engineer your environment to help you? What visual or auditory cues can you use?

Keeping track of your progress and adjusting your strategy along the way are essential to success, so go back to these questions regularly. But precisely how often you must reevaluate your plan is impossible to answer, for just as there is no one-size-fits-all strategy, neither is there a one-size-fits-all timeline.

Taking Time

The timeline itself is twofold: First you have to *give your strategy enough time to work*. Don't forget that you're trying to create new habits or behaviors that will eventually be as instinctive and familiar as the destructive past ones that you're trying to eliminate. You've had years to establish those negative habits, and you can't expect new ones to develop overnight. They can't, and they won't.

Unfortunately, the patience necessary in this quest for self-change can be a rare commodity for adults with ADHD. For many of my clients, the process itself becomes boring, so they don't stick to any system long enough to solidify the new habits they need. Like Amy, they're on to a new plan before letting the original one develop, impulsively feeding their need for distraction by turning their attention elsewhere.

Others are like Mariana, deciding that nothing is right so everything must be wrong. Still others spend inordinate amounts of time developing elaborate plans but never invest any time in carrying them out. The plan grabs their attention, but working the plan doesn't hold it.

But once you've accepted the importance of patience in executing your plan—in the premise that change takes time—you can consider the second aspect of the coaching timeline: *taking time to evaluate the plan*.

Just as many of my clients speak with me weekly, you, as your own coach, can make weekly appointments with yourself to assess how your plan is working. As you ask yourself the questions in your notebook, however, be aware of how much time has passed since you began working the plan. Evaluating weekly does not mean changing strategies weekly. Change will not happen overnight. Give the plan time to work before you change it.

Although I want you to expect the best as you self-coach, I also want you to be prepared for the frustration that will likely set in. If, for example, you get sidetracked from your goal, use the evaluation time to consider the following questions:

Am I repeating an old pattern of not giving something enough time?

Do I want to quit out of sheer boredom?

Is wanting to quit a warning sign of a repeated pattern I fall into?

Am I separating the *action* from my *ADHD brain*? In other words, is it my ADHD causing the plan not to work, or is it the plan itself?

How can I make the plan more enticing for me to follow without compromising the entire plan?

How does my plan support my mission statement?

"I've finally learned something that has helped me evaluate my progress," my client Tim told me recently. "I actually made a sign to hang in my office and another one to hang over my desk at home, so every day I look at it and say the words out loud as a reminder: 'Progress Is Likely to Be Uncertain and Unsteady and Slow.' I think it helps, because I can feel myself becoming more patient."

Tim was on to something when he learned to acknowledge and accept delayed gratification, an almost alien concept in today's "give it to me now!" culture. Setting the words in front of him was also wise, for the repetition of his belief that change takes time deepened his commitment to taking time to achieve his goals. His habit of *stating that progress takes time* became the habit of actually *giving progress time*.

And, as success often begets success, the patience Tim learned to practice has begun to manifest itself elsewhere. Understanding that he has to think long-term, he has designed a yearlong plan of what he wants to accomplish and monthly, weekly, and daily strategies to get there. "Now I plan each day the night before," he said, "so that the day's plan will get me closer to the goals I set up for myself for the year. I hold myself accountable to complete the day's plan. I don't put more on the plan than I'm confident I can fully complete. I regularly revise my annual plan to reflect my current position. I do my level best to live and work by design—I define it, time-frame it, and visualize the steps. I never stop evaluating the procedures I've chosen."

Tim's commitment to his goal, and his commitment to the process of accomplishing it, can and should be your own. Recognize, as he does, that self-management is a journey, and take responsibility for following the long path stretched before you. Keep track of your progress, and evaluate your steps along the way, remembering also to note your triumphs and your strengths in your evaluation.

"I've come to know and trust and love my X-ray vision," Brian said. "It's my competitive secret, my distinctive competency. Every time I see how it works for me, I really believe I can reach the goals I've set. It's my motivator! If I can do X, I feel like I can do Y, even if Z doesn't happen to be working."

Develop the self-awareness to self-initiate change. It's the best way to energize your effort to succeed.

IN THE A-N-S-W-E-R, *EVALUATING THE PLAN* MEANS:
- Taking time to appraise your plan and strategies
- Allowing sufficient time for new strategies to work
- Changing those strategies that don't work by creating new ones based on your strengths
- Continually renewing your commitment to the plan
- Affirming your success along the way
- Energizing your effort

R. REPEAT AND REINFORCE

Several months ago, after a speech I delivered about the benefits of ADHD coaching, I was asked if any one part of the **A-N-S-W-E-R** is more important than another. "Is there any one part a client absolutely can't skip?" an audience member wanted to know.

Fully aware that those with ADHD often look for shortcuts when the road ahead seems long and uneven, I answered immediately, "They're all important." Then I added just as quickly, "But one step does need emphasis. The most critical thing in the long run has to be repeating the process continually."

Unfortunately, repeating the process is also the most difficult.

People with ADHD have practiced masking it and pretending it's otherwise, "overcompensating and going overboard," as one client put it, "to exceed others' expectations." How easy it becomes, then, to forget a lifetime of struggling when a strategy has worked once! How easy, how natural, to want to bask—and linger—in the pleasure of that momentary success!

But if you're going to succeed at achieving those goals you've articulated—if you're finally going to love the way you live—then you cannot let down your guard. Instead of becoming complacent about meeting one goal, build on your success and set another goal. Unfortunately, people with ADHD have memory lapses. They easily forget the consequences of the past and the goal for the future. When a plan or structure works, they ease off, thinking, "I don't need this anymore. I've solved my problem. I'm fine now," and they stop using new strategies. They slip back into old habits, the bad habits they had been determined to leave behind.

As I remind my clients over and over again, quitting after one success is not how permanent change occurs. Remember that you're trying to create new habits, new automatic responses to replace years of self-defeating behaviors. Remember Tim's daily repetition, "Progress is likely to be uncertain and unsteady and slow." It's hard work to do so, but effort is everything!

You have to know that and accept that, and just as important, you have to develop, like Tim, the habit of repetition. Repeating and reinforcing strategies is critical to your success. The idea is to use the success of meeting small challenges to stimulate the push for meeting larger ones.

What is the **A-N-S-W-E-R,** then, in self-coaching?

Acknowledge that you need to repeat the process, narrow in on how you can remain vigilant, set up strategies to remind you that you will forget, know that it takes work, work, and more work, continually evaluate how you are doing, and repeat, repeat, repeat!

"To stay motivated, focused, and self-aware," one client told me, "I drew up a list of beliefs as I was thinking about my mission statement. I try to read them every day when I have my morning coffee, but I also have copies in my office, in my briefcase, even folded up in my wallet just in case, so I have no excuse for not repeating them. It's been more than two years and I haven't missed a single day."

Accepting not only his ADHD, but the responsibility for addressing and managing it as well, Michael reminds himself daily of his goals and his plan to achieve them. "It helps shift the constant self-doubt to a confidence in my ability to see patterns, things, behaviors," he said. "Doing even little things like this consistently gives me that confidence. But I refuse to fool myself by thinking I can't slip back. That's why, no matter how hokey it might seem, I affirm my goals and my mission statement every day."

With a belief in possibility, with vigilance and effort and an iron will to succeed, you can commit to changing your life. But remember why you inquired about self-coaching in the first place. If you have ADHD, you tend to live in the present, forgetting both the pain of past behaviors and the goals of future success. You really have to repeat the A-N-S-W-E-R process so that self-coaching will work. Without it, change will be difficult—if not impossible—to self-initiate.

IN THE A-N-S-W-E-R, *REPEAT AND REINFORCE* MEANS:

- Acknowledge once again that you have ADHD
- Remind yourself that your ADHD will not go away
- Narrow the focus again to one or two key issues
- Strategize again, build strength-based structures
- Ritualize changes, create an additional routine
- Watch that you do not let up, take shortcuts, or get lazy when working the plan
- Evaluate again, chart how much progress you've made

The Big Picture

"I accept ADHD as an explanation, not an excuse," Michael told me, "and I take full responsibility for my life. I strive each day to manage the negative aspects and accentuate the positive." But Michael didn't tell just me. He tells himself, daily, as part of his mission statement, as one of the foundations on which his growing self-confidence rests.

I mention it because with all the emphasis on compensating for ADHD symptoms, I don't want you to lose sight of the positive ways in which your ADHD might manifest itself. Denial of your ADHD may be the "untenable, indefensible position" Tim knows it is, but so is denial of the wonderful qualities that make you who you are. "I'm unique," Tim can now state out loud. "I love my spontaneous, impulsive nature. I love that I let myself be randomly kind each day!"

If you're going to succeed at self-coaching—if you're going to let the **A-N-S-W-E-R** work—I urge you to be as kind to yourself as I try to be to my clients, as resolutely and stubbornly and firmly kind. "The relationship is everything," Mariana said when I asked her to evaluate our progress together. "You believe in me. That's what I need . . . that's what you provide."

As your own coach, you're in a relationship with yourself now. Make that relationship work. Believe in yourself. Have the heart and the vision to propel yourself forward.

PART II

Coaching the ADHD Brain

Among the rituals of my childhood, Sunday morning meant ten o'clock church. It meant prayer and sanctity and family togetherness, my parents and siblings and I dressed in our finest and seated at the front of the congregation, all eyes and ears on the preacher exhorting us toward salvation.

My own salvation was always in doubt, however, for if my father's predictions proved accurate, the Pearly Gates would surely be locked by the time I showed up to claim my reward.

"What's wrong with you, Nancy?" he'd be yelling as the rest of the family piled into the car at 9:45. Then, honking the horn in rhythm with each syllable, he'd continue to threaten and coax me from the house, where I remained half-asleep and half-dressed and fully in dread of my fate.

"I'm giving you exactly sixty seconds to get out here," he'd yell, a prelude to the punishment he'd promise next. "Not one more second or you're grounded."

Most Sundays I'd manage to scramble into the backseat with a

second or two to spare, and off the family would go, picture perfect and prompt as we pulled up in front of the church. Once I
was inside, it wasn't the preacher's voice or the holy men's choir
that echoed in my ears. It was the familiar strains of my father's
lament, the aching reminder of his wishing and worrying, that
even the angels themselves could not hope to drown out. "What's
going to become of you, Nancy? You'll never get anywhere if
you're always going to be late. I wish I knew what to do with you.
I wish I knew how to help."

I wish I could say that the look of concern in my father's eyes
or the desperate love that prompted his punishments or even the
groundings and phoneless nights were cure enough for my perpetual lateness. I wish I could say that I woke up one morning
before the alarm startled me from my dreams; that I was early,
early, early for breakfast and school; that I never again had to
sneak into class and slip into my seat just before the teacher
reached the last of the alphabetical names on her attendance
list—Young, Nancy.

I wish I could also say that years later, I never disappointed my
friends who were waiting for me; that at last they could stop
counting on *not* counting on me; that this was college, after all,
and of course I could be *counted on*—to keep my commitments,
to complete my work, to do what I said I would do.

But it wasn't that easy.

And it certainly would never be automatic.

Learning as much as I could about ADHD and acknowledging
that perpetual lateness was more than an exasperating personality quirk were the only things that ultimately allowed me to stop
feeling terrible and to start changing my ways. Once I finally understood what was going on with my mind and why, I came up
with strategies to address a real ADHD issue, measuring time.

When I was diagnosed with ADHD, I manifested many of the
classic symptoms. I was often distracted. I'd have a million things

going simultaneously but have a hard time following through on any of them. I was impulsive and restless and easily bored by routine.

You might say that I was like most people diagnosed with ADHD. I exhibited a multitude of troublesome behaviors, and as much as I wanted to rush in and conquer them all at once, I had to understand that I couldn't attack everything. I had to highlight and concentrate on one symptom at a time. And because time mismanagement was at the root of so many of my problems, I identified that particular deficit as most important for me.

The problem of time mismanagement, however, did not—and to this day does not—exist in a vacuum. Like any other ADHD issue, it's part of a whole, part and parcel of the many behaviors caused by my ADHD.

But to illustrate how the **A-N-S-W-E-R** works for specific ADHD symptoms, and to provide specific strategies to address those symptoms, the following chapters present stories of various clients, whose names and identifying particulars have been changed to maintain confidentiality but whose coaching journeys are portrayed as accurately as possible.

Each chapter highlights one particular ADHD symptom, but this is in no way to suggest that anyone is a single "ADHD type." It is merely a way of narrowing the focus, one of the critical steps in self-coaching. I want you to see, in depth, how real strategies are applied to real problems.

Let me stress again that *no one is a single "ADHD type."* Most people with the disorder manifest several ADHD characteristics simultaneously, one or two of which may be more readily apparent or troublesome than others. Highlighting one symptom at a time is simply a tool for me to teach you the process of self-coaching. I hope that by recognizing yourself in some of the descriptions that follow, you'll learn something about changing your own life.

It's true that to address my own issue with measuring time, I've developed strategies involving calendars and clocks, and it's also true that many people, especially clients, can now count on me. Before he died, my father could count on me, too, and could celebrate with me the control over lateness that I'd managed to attain. "Look what you've accomplished," he'd often tell me, his voice swelling with pride and his eyes misting. "And you've done it all on your own," he'd insist for good measure, until I'd feel as proud and weepy as he.

But whatever I've accomplished as an adult is true only because of the commitment I've made to the same advice I give you. In my own life—in my daily life—I follow the steps of the **A-N-S-W-E-R,** and like others who experience setbacks and frustration, I dig a little deeper into my well of resolve when I face my own. I read my mission statement, and I repeat my daily goals.

With years of practice behind me, I've learned that I cannot, for a single day, let down my guard. But I celebrate my victories, too, and then I use these successes as motivation to move forward. Once I've done one thing, I believe I can do another. That's when I repeat the process of strategizing and evaluating, working the plan toward the new goal I've set.

Changing your life is a daily struggle. It is for me, it is for my clients, and it will be for you.

But as I said on the first page of this book, it's also possible, and it's surely worthwhile. I offer my clients' stories now as proof.

CHAPTER 5

Time Mismanagement

I was almost thirty by the time I was diagnosed with ADHD, which I think made me fortunate in a number of respects. For one thing, I had an adult's appreciation of the stakes involved in addressing the problem. With a bachelor's degree behind me and a master's degree ahead, I was extremely motivated to change the ADHD behavior that had plagued my life to that point.

I was also confident that I could escape the potential conse-quences of professional failure that undiagnosed ADHD adults might face. I knew, after all, that the strategies and structures I put in place as a student could ultimately transfer to the profes-sional life still in front of me. By the time I began working with a coach, I had learned enough about ADHD and my own struggles to prevent them from interfering with my life's work. Mostly, I had learned to manage the time mismanagement that had de-fined my earlier years.

Maybe that helps to explain the particular empathy I felt when Claire, one of the first clients with whom I worked as an "official" coach, narrated a story eerily familiar in its broader sense to the one I intimately knew. Like the earlier me, Claire could not seem to capture the essence of time. Estimating how long a given task would take was virtually impossible, and plan as she might, she continually disappointed both herself and others by failing to translate promises into reality. Family, friends, and now professional associates were increasingly affected by her inability to manage time, and Claire understood that neither they nor she could continue to live with her chronic dysfunction.

But it was Lucy, her thirteen-year-old daughter, who had unwittingly challenged Claire into seeking help. "I know I can't depend on you," Lucy had said, so matter-of-factly that Claire was startled by the power of Lucy's indictment. "And you know it, too." The judgment and disapproval of others had been difficult enough for Claire to process, but the condemnation of Lucy had been more than she could bear.

Interestingly, Claire had believed after her recent divorce that leaving the investment firm where she'd worked for ten years to begin a private practice from home would be helpful. As she saw it, the benefits were clear. She could finally eliminate the stressful office environment she'd blamed for the collapse of her marriage. She could give her clients independent advice when she didn't have to consider partners' views. She could set her own schedule, she could be flexible when she needed to be, she could spend as much time with her daughter as Lucy requested or required. Her problems, in other words, could disappear with the commute that she'd also leave behind.

What Claire never considered, however, was that the high-pressure environment from which she wanted to escape had served as the structure she really needed to keep track of time. "I felt like I was on an assembly line," she said of the timelines and deadlines and partners' demands that made up a typical day at the office. "And I couldn't take it for one more second."

What she didn't say—what she didn't understand until later—was that the external order imposed by colleagues had been compensating for her internal deficiency managing schedules. She had been successful, in other words, to the extent that others had been programming time for her. Although she could admit it only grudgingly at first, even her ex-husband had provided her with the time management she couldn't provide for herself. His reminders about when things needed to be done hadn't been nagging after all, Claire came to realize. They'd been a survival technique to help her, and the family, function. And although she swore that she was "on top of things" and "great at making my own schedules," she became painfully aware once she was in her own practice that all the planning in the world did not translate to planning *carefully*.

She was "tunneling" into projects, she said, and before she knew it, hours would pass. What might begin as a simple check of one fact on the Internet could easily turn into three days of information seeking. Left to her own devices, she faced increasing pressure to do what was less and less possible for her to do—work within an established time frame, setting and observing the parameters herself. It seemed her business was doomed before it had a chance to survive.

Claire didn't know if the most important relationship in her life, the relationship with Lucy, would survive, either. She frequently let Lucy down, forgetting to be where she had promised to be at various appointed times. Soccer practice pickup, the mother-daughter school luncheon, the class play performance: Claire couldn't get any of it right. "Some of my friends don't even think I have a mother!" Lucy cried after a particularly bitter disappointment. "They think I made you up. What's wrong with you?"

Desperate to change her life, to keep it from unraveling completely, Claire turned to coaching for an answer.

The A-N-S-W-E-R for Claire

"I'll do anything to change," Claire declared in our first coaching session.

A. ACKNOWLEDGING THE ADHD

Only by understanding the implications of ADHD could Claire acknowledge how it had been functioning in her life—that the condition itself had elevated what might be an easily explained annoyance for most people into a serious problem for her.

Juggling the responsibilities of a job, a family, and a household can be trying for anyone, not just for a mom or a home office worker. It's easy to forget to run an errand or make a phone call, and it's easy to run late for an appointment now and then. It becomes a far more significant issue, however, when mismanagement of time becomes pervasive enough to affect your job and your personal life, crippling your self-esteem and dismantling your dreams along the way. Claire had to admit that chronic lateness—always overestimating what she could accomplish in any given time period—could not be explained away as a personality quirk. Neither could it be ignored.

By acknowledging her ADHD, and by understanding the connection between her inability to measure time and the neurobiological disorder at its root, Claire could dismiss the instinctive emotional response—*I'm so stupid, I'm so undependable, I'm a terrible mother*—on which she had relied for years and replace it with an objectively designed strategy to address the problem. All the apologies in the world, all the tears and accusations and pleas and promises, would do nothing to alter her sense of time. But separating herself from her problem and taking action would.

Claire exhibited the same self-loathing to which many ADHD clients are prone. In addition to the guilt and embarrassment that frequently reduced her to tears, she'd often experienced a debilitating frustration when she couldn't accomplish what she initially set out to do. She was blaming a lack of ability within herself because she couldn't blame a lack of time. "I can't ever do anything in a normal amount of time," she said. "I don't know where the hours go."

Like other clients, Claire could free up an entire day, even two or three days, to complete a project, only to find no time to finish at the end. Sometimes, she admitted, she'd waited until the last minute to start the task. Other times she'd given in to diversions. With no prior warning, weeding the garden or cleaning out her closet could suddenly lure her off course and soak up her time.

"I'll just do this 'quickly' before I start to work on my . . ." had become a way of life for Claire, but her real issue was not having a conceptual framework for judging time. Unfortunately, she could never see the full picture. She couldn't clearly envision the details involved in performing a task or completing an activity, even a simple one like shopping or folding the laundry.

Already late to pick up Lucy, for example, Claire sometimes decided that in between home and the soccer field she could mail packages at the post office and drop off clothes at the dry cleaner's. Inconceivable as it might sound in the light of past experience, she would nevertheless believe it possible to "just run by" these places on the way. To make matters worse, she'd often have to go back into the house for forgotten keys or a wallet, and she'd be immediately sidetracked by a phone call, never getting to the errands or to her daughter, whose pickup was the actual task in the first place. "My ex-husband used to say I could do the same thing with the same results ninety-nine times in a row, and I'd still be surprised and crying and apologizing the hundredth time. I can't stand it anymore," she told me.

Acknowledging her ADHD and understanding its effects on her ability to estimate time eventually helped Claire focus on solving the problem, which in turn helped eliminate her chronic sense of failure. Because she came to understand that her ADHD would not magically disappear, that it would be part of her forever, she learned despite the setbacks to address it, directing her energy toward the issues and away from self-blame.

Discovering the Root of Time Mismanagement

Claire's real problem was that although she could visualize the completion of any given activity, she could not anticipate the actual passage of time carrying out details of the activity, a phenomenon I know firsthand. Like many of my clients, I can always visualize the ending. I saw myself graduating from Harvard, and it happened; I saw myself finishing the Boston Marathon, and I did. And when a business trip or vacation is imminent, I can also visualize myself at the airport, presenting my ID at the counter, walking to the gate, boarding the plane, and taking my seat.

But what I cannot visualize are the details in between, like packing, leaving the house, driving to the airport, and parking the car, which means I'm always running late for flights and racing onto the plane at the last possible second. Somehow I can't slow down enough to break tasks up into blocks of time. I can't anticipate that time actually passes as I take the individual steps between planning for the trip and walking onto the plane.

For individuals with ADHD, much of the time mismanagement problem centers on this inability to see themselves all the way through an activity, a project, or even a simple task. Not making plans at all, making unrealistic plans, overplanning, and failing to stick to plans all contribute to the problem, and although none are ADHD-specific, they're definitely magnified for those who have ADHD.

N. NARROWING THE FOCUS

"Look at this list," Claire said a few weeks into our coaching. "No wonder I'm such a failure." Then she asked, her voice a frustrated mix of sadness and shame, "Who could stand having a wife or mother like me? Who'd want me to manage their investments?"

Claire's self-evaluation sheet had revealed multiple outcomes of her inability to manage time, and the length of the list was daunting to her. But narrowing the focus was easy on one level: Whatever other ADHD symptoms she might be manifesting, most of the negative effects she hoped to eliminate stemmed from her issues with time.

The more difficult aspect of narrowing the focus for Claire was learning to self-monitor, which had been alien to her up to this point. Like most people who mismanage time, she had never looked objectively at how, all plans to the contrary, she wound up off course—how she could be hanging curtains in the bathroom, for example, when she was supposed to be cheering for Lucy on the soccer sideline; how she could return from a quick noon post office run six hours later, unmailed bills still on the dashboard of the car and an investment prospectus still unread.

"Oh, that happens to me sometimes," most people have probably said, but most people—the vast majority of the population who don't struggle with ADHD—haven't experienced time mismanagement as a way of life. Most people realize when they've been sidetracked. Most people can look at the clock and readjust.

If you're like Claire, a key to making progress is self-observation, which means monitoring your actions to pinpoint what takes you off course. Claire was often lured from her goal by things she'd never planned for, things she'd never built into her day, timeless things, in a sense, because she hadn't considered doing them at all. She had never considered looking objectively at how her hours "disappeared."

Just as in other coaching strategies, there's something of a paradox inherent in self-monitoring. It takes time, a precious and rare commodity if you mismanage time, to observe literally every activity, significant or otherwise, in which you engage. It takes time to list and to study what you do during the course of a day, and it takes time to anticipate distractions that could lead you astray. It takes the time that people who mismanage time think they don't have. But since *taking* time is the only way to *manage* time, you have to commit to the process if you're going to change your life.

For one thing, by monitoring how you spend your time, you'll eliminate the denial that characterizes so many clients, who can't understand where the time went. Once she saw in writing that "just five more minutes" in the garden had turned to two hours turning compost, Claire could no longer dismiss as "No way!" the amount of time her attention had been diverted from her primary goal. When she saw in writing that the one hour she'd allotted for research of an investment point had turned to six hours reading about the latest billionaires, she could no longer deny the hyperfocusing that had kept her off track.

Once she began to monitor how she spent time, Claire also learned to prevent likely distractions before they emerged. It wasn't easy to become self-observant, but by asking herself the following questions, she inched her way toward the control of life she had sought, learning to feel better about herself in the process:

- What might get in the way of my primary commitment?
- What can I do to stop myself from engaging in the distraction?
- What can I do to prevent the distraction in the first place?

S. STRATEGIZING

Claire needed to create strength-based strategies for estimating and measuring time, strategies based on routine and structure and on a means of measuring the completion time of an activity within that structure. At the same time, though, she had to avoid the trap of premature gratification—spending so much time on planning that she never got to the work.

Clearly, there's nothing wrong, and there's much right, with making detailed plans. But individuals with ADHD can derive so much pleasure from the planning itself that they believe they've been committed to the action as well. They feel in control when they see the schedule they've devised, and they equate the time spent drawing it up with time spent carrying it out.

Planning

To keep herself honest about where her time was actually going, Claire established a defined start and stop time for planning the day's activities, setting an alarm to signal the end of a planning session. Then she printed the plan she'd created, placed it in front of her, and checked off each step of the task as she completed it.

Detailed planning was difficult for Claire, because, despite making elaborate plans in the past, she was not used to making workable ones, plans that allowed for less obvious details, the ones she couldn't "see" because of her ADHD. She could envision calling a client, and she could envision discussing a mutual fund he'd been considering, but she couldn't envision discussing the details of various asset allotments and turnover ratios and performance charts that her client would want her to explain, which made completing business in the time she originally allotted impossible.

Claire literally had to learn a new way of thinking with her ADHD in mind. She had to acknowledge and accept that underestimating the amount of time needed for a particular activity is normal, especially when she was beginning the process. I tell my clients that much of what they initially plan is going to be more a wish list than reality, but that if they stick with the process, they'll learn from experience how to be more realistic in allotting time to task.

Learning how to plan properly was tedious and anxiety-producing work in the beginning, and Claire admitted to "crumpling up the stupid paper and throwing it against the wall" on many days, but the satisfaction she began to derive from marking accomplishments eventually surpassed the agitation of paying attention to details.

Timers

Claire began to use timers to her advantage. She bought a countdown timer with a particularly piercing buzz and used it to keep track of the "just a few more minutes" that had been throwing her off course. As soon as she began a task that wasn't specifically spelled out on her plan for the day, she hit the timer, which was always set for five minutes. Trial and error had also taught her to place the timer slightly out of reach. She hated its incessant buzzing, so she couldn't ignore its reminder to get back on task. The physical act of leaving the specific spot in which she was working and moving to the timer to shut it off made her more likely to disengage from the impulsive activity and get back to the one on her plan.

Bookends and Anchors

To restore the sense of continuity of time that her colleagues had provided at the firm, Claire needed to create home rituals and routines that centered on time.

The first thing she did was to create "bookends" for each day by getting up and going to bed at the same set times. The routine, which was relatively easy to establish because she could follow Lucy's existing schedule, provided a rudimentary sense of structure and a familiarity with the time at which these activities took place. She also set a time to eat lunch each day and a time to exercise by walking the dog immediately after.

By setting structures for a few basic needs—sleep, food, exercise—Claire became conscious of scheduled activities throughout her day. The structures in turn became "anchors" for each day, providing her a sense of how the day broke down into segments. By becoming aware of when the next activity in her routine would begin, Claire ultimately learned to anticipate what she could or couldn't do in a given time period, which made her less inclined to begin tasks that would take her off track.

Multiple Alarms and Backup

To reinforce the concept of "bookends" and "anchors," and to help her become more consistent in her daily activities, Claire set several alarms to sound at various parts of the day—at 8:50, the signal to report into her home office at 9:00; at 11:50, a reminder to stop for lunch at noon; and at 3:50, the cue to pick up Lucy at 4:05. She knew, for example, that if she weren't sitting at her desk at 9:00 a.m., she would probably be doing something "unplanned." The alarm served as a warning to report to her office. More important, the alarm focused her on adhering to the schedule she had planned.

Borrowing from her "planning" strategy, Claire set her alarms in inconvenient places that she would have to walk to in order to silence them. Her office was near the kitchen, so she placed the alarm in the hallway she'd have to use on the way to lunch. Any temptation to hunker down and skip lunch—the hyperfocusing to which she often fell prey—would be offset by the piercing signal she couldn't ignore. By arranging her environment, Claire helped herself set a routine.

W. WORKING THE PLAN

Claire had initially placed a large clock by her computer. Unfortunately, she rarely, if ever, looked at it. She also wrote out endless to-do lists. She didn't look at them, either.

I gave Claire credit for trying, but the visual cues she was using clearly weren't designed for her strengths. She agreed to my suggestion of auditory cues like alarms or music. When the timers and buzzers began to work, she decided to try a wristwatch with multiple alarms, setting them to sound every hour so that she could hear the passing of time. By knowing that a particular amount of time had elapsed, she could then compare her printed plan with what she had actually accomplished and adjust her actions accordingly. This clocking in and clocking out made her accountable for completing tasks.

E. EVALUATING THE PLAN

Like so many clients, Claire had been stuck in a cycle of failed responses to the symptoms dragging her down. Using new strategies to address her ADHD symptoms was a revelation.

Evaluating what she was doing was also a striking, and difficult, new concept. It wasn't easy for Claire to abandon her big clock and her myriad Post-it notes, none of which helped her manage time. By nature she was rigid, she told me, and she tended to adhere to an idea, even in the face of negative results.

Over time, she learned to match her coping strategies to her strengths. Realizing that she responded to auditory cues, she added more and more ideas to her repertoire. She set the alarm on her clock radio to a music station, for example, and turned its volume so high that she'd have to turn it down as soon as it sounded. She deliberately placed the radio on the highest bookshelf in the front room near the door, forcing her to move from wherever she happened to be at the moment to turn the radio off. Then she would immediately grab the keys she had placed on the same shelf and leave to pick up Lucy.

None of it came naturally to her, but evaluating her progress was worth the effort when, several years later, her independent business had grown substantially. The effort proved especially worthwhile when Lucy volunteered her mother as chaperone on her senior class trip. "You're the best, Mom," she told Claire. "I can't wait to have you with us in Washington."

Telling me about Lucy, Claire reminded me of the mission statement she had composed shortly after we began coaching. "I will live my life in a way that makes me, and my daughter, proud," it had read.

No wonder Claire was crying when she told me.

R. REPEATING THE PLAN

Like any other individual with ADHD, Claire had to remember, "I've been down this road before!" She had to remember that she could be her own worst enemy if she didn't continue to work her plan.

The only way for her, or anybody, to do so is to repeat, repeat, repeat. Claire learned to keep the plan in place, regardless. She didn't always succeed, but she learned to accept inevitable setbacks as part of being human.

"I Can't Do Everything in One Day!" Lucy had painted years ago on a sign that still hangs in Claire's office. Claire admitted that she doesn't always remember to read it, but she did learn to follow Lucy's cue. To this day, those words are as necessary to Claire's functioning as the sustaining love the words imply.

"Say it, Mom," Lucy always begins, whenever they talk on the phone.

To which Claire always replies, laughing, "I can't do everything in one day!"

No one can. It is with Claire's blessing that I share that belief with you.

Strategies for Those Who Mismanage Time

Like Claire, you have to accept that your time management challenges are more profound than those of most people. You have ADHD, after all, and you're never going to change that fact, but you can change its effects on your life by developing strategies to manage it.

Perhaps you can adopt Claire's strategies, the ones that

WITHIN THE BRAIN: IT'S ABOUT TIME
by John J. Ratey, M.D.

In the brain, the attention system and motor system are closely allied in their development and operation. Both, in part, affect our ability to keep time and to keep our inner experience feeling continuous.

The frontal lobe—more specifically, the dorsolateral prefrontal cortex—is commonly called the brain's CEO, which governs all our "executive functions," including time management and working memory. Owing to the ADHD brain's underarousal in the prefrontal area, the ability to measure and estimate time is almost always compromised.

In addition to the frontal lobes, there are two areas critical to attention and motor timing that impinge on the struggles with time that people with ADHD have. The cerebellum, which I call the "rhythm and blues" area, helps in making our movements smooth and rhythmic. Disturbances in this area can challenge a person's ability to "be in flow," and they experience time as choppy or discontinuous.

The other area is the basal ganglia, an area deep inside the brain thought mainly to handle movements, especially automatic movement. In the attention system, it is likened to an "automatic transition," helping us to shift smoothly from idea to idea. Malfunctions in this area can result in "getting stuck" in thought for hours or being unable to "shift" without the help of external reminders.

worked—*bookends* and *anchors, timers, multiple alarms*—or, as Claire told me, anything that is number based. Or perhaps you might prefer the ones that didn't work for her but might for you—*clocks, Post-it notes,* and *calendars.*

Through trial and error, clients have created all kinds of strategies, some of which might also give you ideas.

SCHEDULE BREAKS

Hyperfocusing can create havoc when it comes to time management. Not only does it mean that, with no regard to priorities, you'll wind up doing one particular project at the expense of others, but it can also contribute to low blood sugar and fatigue. Taking distinct breaks will allow you to rejuvenate and to improve the quality of the work you've already begun. The point is not to abandon what you've been doing, but to return to it with renewed energy and focus.

DESIGNATE STOP AND START TIMES

Designating stop and start times means terminating one activity and beginning another—stopping work on task A and starting task B.

If you don't designate stop times for activities, projects and tasks can "bleed" into each other because time seems open-ended, which is not helpful for someone with ADHD.

USE THE "HALF IN HALF IN HALF" RULE

Chances are, the time that you actually allot to any given project is often "wishful thinking," a setup for failure.

But there's a "golden rule" that can help you plan more effectively. For any given time frame, take half of any given task, then cut that in half, and cut that in half again. In other words, *plan to do only a fraction of what you would normally set out to do.*

Using this "half in half in half" formula will help you maintain boundaries. And being more realistic in your time estimates, you won't be setting yourself up for failure. Set yourself up for success instead, and watch that success multiply!

MAKE AN APPOINTMENT WITH YOURSELF

If you keep appointments with others, why not make—and keep—appointments with yourself? Designate "home office hours" to pay bills, for example, or mark "Tuesdays at Ten" to plan the weekly meals.

Scheduling time in this way can help you see necessary activities and the time in which you'll do them in the concrete terms all individuals with ADHD need.

MEASURE TIME

For three days, write down how long it takes to do routine things—taking your shower, for example, or feeding the dogs. By getting an idea of how long you spend on each, you can learn to calculate the actual time it takes for other activities in your day.

Select four or five simple activities like eating breakfast or making the bed, or the two I mentioned above. In your coaching notebook or file, list the activities next to the left margin of a clean page. Then make three columns across the page, dating each for three successive days.

On each day, use the stopwatch to time the length of each of the activities you listed, not to beat the clock each day, but to see an accurate picture of the time each task takes.

MEASURING TIME
Morning Routine

ACTIVITY	DAY 1—TIME	DAY 2—TIME	DAY 3—TIME
Shower			
Eat breakfast			
Get dressed			
Feed dogs			

While it might seem that you're wasting time by measuring time, you most definitely are not!

Measuring time will help you estimate time in planning your daily schedule. When you make a to-do list, write in some of your daily activities first, knowing how long they should take. Then set an alarm to sound at the time limit you've realistically designated for each specific task. You'll get used to how long the typical, often neglected, aspects of the day take. Then you're more likely to develop the sense of time you need for other things.

HEAR THE PASSING OF TIME

To help you learn how long an hour is, buy a sports watch and set it to beep every hour on the hour. Gradually, by "hearing" the passing of time, you'll become more conscious of not only time, but also the length of an hour. There are many other alternatives if you don't want to use a beeping watch. You can get one that vibrates, or you can use your PDA.

DIVIDE YOUR DAY INTO "QUADRANTS"

Many of my clients don't react well to detailed time management systems, where they put a task next to a time. If you're like them, try dividing your day into different sections and then plug into each section tasks or goals you need to finish. For example, one client divides his day into three blocks: 9–11, 11–2, and 2–5. This way, he knows what things he needs to have accomplished by eleven, two, and five o'clock.

DON'T GET STUCK IN PLANNING

Because the only perfect system for time management is the one that works for *you,* it's up to you to discover your own. To keep myself on track, I have to write out—with a felt-tipped pen on a clean sheet of paper—my top one or two items for the next hour.

I do this for every hour of the day on a clean sheet of paper. I know I go through a lot of paper, but that's the price I pay. It keeps me moving forward, and it keeps my eye on the clock. It works for me, so maybe it will work for you, too!

SEE BOTH THE BIG AND LITTLE PICTURES

Keep a monthly calendar *and* a weekly calendar in tandem. This way, you can keep the larger time frame in full view and monitor your weekly commitments as well. All too often, people with ADHD get stuck in one view or the other.

Another choice is to post several months of calendars, each clearly marked with monthly goals to reinforce the "big picture" and to better "see" your time frame.

BE ACCOUNTABLE FOR YOUR TIME

Tell someone your goals for the day. Sharing what you want to do helps make it happen, so be creative.

Like many of my clients, I work from a home office. One summer when I was having the house painted, I went outside each day and told the painters that by noon I needed to do X, Y, and Z and that if they saw me outside before noon, they should ask me if I had completed X, Y, and Z. They took their job coaching me to heart, and I got a lot done that summer!

CREATE A SYSTEM OF STRUCTURED FLEXIBILITY

Write out on a grid your "fixed" weekly obligations, or create a weekly template. Under the appropriate day and time, place each activity or task. Include work hours, your therapy appointment, your child's soccer game—anything that is *mandatory and recurring*.

Next, designate the remaining time that can be used for doing other tasks—"M, W, F: 9–12 AM and 3–5 PM," for example. These periods will become known as your *"flexible time zones."*

Make lists of all the weekly goals you have: Work on projects ABC, pay bills, grocery shop, do laundry, and so on. Now comes the fun part: Put each goal on a small Post-it note and start to "plug" them into the flexible time zones.

The idea is to create a system of exchanges. If you don't "feel" like doing project B on Monday morning, for example, but you're in the mood to work on the expense report scheduled for Wednesday afternoon, you can exchange these tasks. Just be sure to shuffle the Post-it notes as well, so that the tasks and goals they represent don't disappear.

Your grid might look like this:

MONDAY	TUESDAY	WEDNESDAY	THURSDAY	FRIDAY
9–11 Flex Zone Gym	**9–2 Flex Zone** Project: B	**9–2 Flex Zone** Project: C	7–9 Bible Group	**9–12 Flex Zone** Gym
12:00–1 PM Therapy			**9:30–2 Flex Zone** Meal Planning Groceries	1–2 Weekly Girls Lunch
2:30 PM Kids Soccer	2:30 PM Kids Soccer	2:30 PM Kids Soccer	2:30 PM Kids Soccer	**3–6 Flex Zone** Bills

MONDAY	TUESDAY	WEDNESDAY	THURSDAY	FRIDAY
4–6 Flex Zone	**4–6 Flex Zone**	**4–6 Flex Zone**	**4–6 Flex Zone**	
Project A	Gym	Laundry	Gym	
Dinner	Dinner	Dinner	Dinner	Dinner

LIST OF WEEKLY GOALS

Work on Projects A, B, and C

Pay Bills

Meal Planning

Groceries

Laundry

Gym

Whatever strategies you decide to implement, remember that the key is to evaluate how they are working and to be flexible about changing the ones that aren't working. Take the time to learn to manage time, and like Claire, you can take control of your life!

CHAPTER 6

Procrastination

Being able to help Claire at the start of my career immediately confirmed that I had chosen the right field, but I did wonder if any other client's ADHD struggles would resonate as profoundly with me. I needn't have worried. The ADHD brain doesn't conveniently designate one symptom as the only symptom, and I soon learned that I could relate to almost every problem experienced by those who came to me. So many symptoms overlap that most clients—actually, most adults with ADHD—can say along with me, "Yes, I get it, I've been there, I know what you mean."

In many ways, then, my clients and I are alike. But although the motivation we have all felt to take control of our respective lives might also be equal—we are adults, after all, aware of the stakes involved when a life is out of control—I have been spared the professional consequences that so many of them have endured.

Sam had been moderately successful in the corporate world, his annual reviews attesting to his creative and innovative ideas and his many efforts to improve performance. The caliber of his work, when finally completed, was usually high, and presentations to potential clients were energetic and engaging. People, including his bosses, genuinely liked him.

On the other hand, Sam always appeared on the verge of dismissal. He was disorganized, the reviews noted. He disregarded details and deadlines. He never seemed able to complete his work in advance. Colleagues and even longtime clients and friends had christened him "Last-Second Sam."

Sam had survived the somewhat shaky evaluations of his superiors for more than fifteen years, learning to content himself with minor promotions and occasional bonuses while younger employees surpassed him in both status and compensation. Shortly after he turned forty, however, his life, both professionally and personally, took the first of a series of consequential turns when he attended what he'd expected to be a routine "Meet the Teacher Night."

"Have you considered having Matthew tested?" his son's fifth-grade teacher asked before enumerating to Sam and his wife, Molly, her concerns with Matthew's performance. Matthew was much smarter than his report cards suggested, the teacher said. He could never seem to buckle down to his work, even though he usually knew both the answers and their explanations. He seldom completed classroom assignments, yet the ones he occasionally did finish could be exemplary. And although his energy and his good ideas should have made him a natural leader, he would often say things that alienated his classmates, who would then avoid or tease him.

A Diagnosis for Sam

Several weeks after the parent-teacher conference, ten-year-old Matthew was diagnosed with ADHD, and a few months later, Sam admitted to himself what he had long tried to suppress: For as far back as he could remember, he'd been exhibiting symptoms similar to his son's. Summoning his courage, he decided to seek a diagnosis for himself, and the results were conclusive.

Like Matthew, Sam had ADHD, news he received with mixed feelings.

On the one hand, he could already see a slight, but significant, difference in Matthew's performance once medication had kicked in and his teacher had made adjustments in her planning for Matthew's specific needs. Surely his own performance would improve, Sam thought, and once his bosses noted his increased productivity, a promotion would be forthcoming.

On the other hand, he wanted to keep the diagnosis to himself. Unlike Matthew's teacher, who, upon learning of Matthew's ADHD, was actively seeking to help him in any way she could, no one at work would be accommodating Sam if he didn't disclose his ADHD. It would be up to him to focus and pace himself consistently, something that he clearly did not know how to do, even with the medication he'd been prescribed. (See medication table, page 231.)

One year later, convinced that his history of job performance precluded any possibility of the advancement he desperately wanted, Sam left the only company for which he had worked since earning his master's degree in business administration years earlier. A lifelong friend had suggested they establish a small business of their own, and Sam embraced the opportunity for a fresh start, accepting the offer with enthusiasm.

Unfortunately, co-owning the business with Martin did nothing to change Sam's performance. During periods of high energy, he could still dazzle a client, but just as before, there was little predictability about when such periods would occur. Too often, he gave in to his old ways: lateness with proposals, lateness to meetings, spending too much time on minor projects while major ones sat untouched. If anything, his old habits had become more pronounced without colleagues and superiors to urge him on.

He was in his own start-up company, after all. When the old pressures from above and the nagging dread of being fired and the tight timelines demanded by colleagues all disappeared, so did any semblance of order in Sam's day. House and yard projects that had lain untouched for years appeared suddenly enticing, and Sam joyfully navigated the aisles of Home Depot alongside retirees in their leisure, his thoughts as far from impending deadlines as theirs seemed to be. If he never made it into the office space he and Martin shared downtown, not the slightest twinge of guilt disturbed his day.

Martin provided little impetus for a steadier pace from Sam. Long used to Sam's pulling it off at the last second—as roommate, he had witnessed firsthand Sam's all-nighters—he continued to believe that Sam could, and would, secure the business equivalent of the college A's he had consistently earned. Granting Sam the very freedom to procrastinate that would undermine potential success, he'd assure Sam, "No problem, I know you'll come through."

As bookkeeper for the new venture, Molly had become keenly aware of cash flow and debt, information that exacerbated an already troublesome situation. Her growing discomfort about the couple's financial security had deepened into an anxiety coloring every aspect of the family dynamic, and she became tense and impatient with her husband's "irresponsible ways." Disillusioned and out of answers, she wondered what had become of her role as supportive wife.

For although she loved Sam no less than ever, Molly was increasingly aware of the cost to their relationship that his perpetual procrastinating, and his perpetual presence, had exacted. Even worse than the broken swing and the chipped paint, the ripped screens and the sagging floorboards—all the glaring messes that she had tolerated for years—were his recent compulsions, now that he and Martin were their own bosses, to take care of them. Yes, she blamed Sam for failing to do "what every other husband around here does," but neither was there any joy when he finally did. "Why would you choose now?" she demanded one Sunday afternoon as Sam sawed happily away at oak branches dangling overhead. "Don't you have a major presentation tomorrow morning?"

Startled out of sleep that night by a voice from the next room, Molly found Sam rehearsing the pitch he'd be delivering six hours later. "You can't keep working this way, Sam," she cried. "This is no good. What in the world are we going to do?"

Soon after, Sam called about coaching.

The A-N-S-W-E-R for Sam

A. ACKNOWLEDGING THE ADHD

Like many other adults with ADHD, Sam had spent his life developing both the habit of procrastination and the accompanying, finely tuned tactics that nurtured it. Coaching could help him develop new habits, I promised, but it would be up to him to acknowledge the role ADHD was playing in his life.

Sam knew he had ADHD, but for the most part, his knowledge ended there. Once Matthew had been diagnosed, Molly had been on a personal quest to understand as much as she could about how ADHD was affecting her son, but she and Sam had rarely discussed it. For one thing, Molly saw Matthew as more in need of her help than Sam, so she concentrated her efforts on her child's ADHD, not her husband's. She also wanted Sam to focus on one thing only. It was enough for him to concentrate on work, she told him, especially after he and Martin had begun their partnership. There would be time enough to learn more about his ADHD once the business became profitable.

But if he were going to change the behavior that had led him to me in the first place, Sam could not simply state, "I have ADHD," and expect life to take care of itself. It wouldn't happen that way.

The Art of Procrastination

Who among us doesn't love the luxury of an occasional lazy afternoon, putting off till tomorrow what we might have done today!

We all do, of course, but when people with ADHD procrastinate, they aren't feeling momentarily lazy or giving in to a harmless, well-earned need to unwind. Procrastinating might qualify as a justifiable indulgence or a rare, sweet choice for the majority of people without ADHD, but for those living with it, there is nothing sweet about it. It comes layered with guilt and humiliation and an intuitive sense that you are letting others down.

By acknowledging his ADHD, Sam learned to admit that, for him, procrastination was a significant problem with a biological base, not an occasional reward for serious and consistent work or even the result of a mood swing now and then. And although he could learn to compensate for it, he could never change the biology in which his procrastination was rooted.

Quite simply, he would never have the freedom of choice about certain issues that people without ADHD have. His choices were limited to what he could do to compensate for what his brain propelled him to do, not to the neurological structure of the brain itself. His ADHD wouldn't go away, but the way he behaved because of it could. First, he would have to plan his compensatory strategies. Once they began to work, he could practice, practice, practice until they became, at last, a part of his brain's machinery.

Being A-Historic

Sam's ADHD meant that his continual procrastinating was intertwined with both his ability to forget past actions and consequences and his inability to think beyond the moment, what I call being "a-historic." His brain's lack of working memory—its *not* remembering—meant he easily forgot about not only dead-lines, but also the consequences of missing those deadlines. Trapped as he was in the present, Sam was unable to hold in mind the memory of what had happened every other time he had put something off. Instead, he focused on what was in front of him at any given moment—dead branches in need of removal, for example—instead of on what past experience should have been reminding him—*if you are unprepared with a presentation, you will lose the client, whose business you sorely need.*

By distinguishing what was biological about his procrastinat-ing and what was merely adaptive, Sam could begin to make the changes he and Molly needed. In other words, by learning to change the elements of behavior that were within his control, he could change the outcomes as well, improving the areas of life that had been the source of personal failure and marital discord.

Clearly, Sam wasn't trying to frustrate Molly by repairing the porch swing when he should have been meeting with Martin. He wasn't trying to humiliate himself or his partner by forgetting about a client waiting for an answer. He wasn't lying when over and over again he said he was sorry for his behavior. But stuck in a different moment, he was forgetting the promises he had made of "never again, never." If he could identify what caused him to for-get, he could create strategies to remember past consequences.

Productive Procrastination

One of the problems for Sam was that he could easily ignore his original goals and get lost in some other activity, usually some-thing more fun or trivial than what he'd initially set out to do. He knew that he would eventually throw himself into work that needed to be done, so he actually enjoyed this ability to hyperfo-cus. "I used to drive Martin nuts when we were in college," he ad-mitted. "Martin would work at his papers way in advance while I played soccer or basketball, but I'd always be the one getting the

A's by doing the whole thing in one day. I just wouldn't sleep the night before it was due. I'm surprised Martin still even talks to me. He wouldn't get any sleep those nights, either, but hey, it worked for me."

On the other hand, Sam knew that his old habit was beginning to prove his undoing. "I couldn't believe Molly was so mad," he said, as he related the story of the hanging branches. "I thought she'd be glad I was finally cutting them down. She'd been after me for months, she was always complaining that somebody could get hurt if one of the big ones fell during a storm." Then he sighed. "Who knew?"

I knew. I knew because I'd seen many other clients do exactly what he was doing.

This "productive procrastination" is a popular survival tactic among my clients. They enjoy *feeling* busy, and they fool themselves into thinking that of course they *are* busy, they're *not* procrastinating, they're getting so much accomplished, so how could anyone say they're not working? They delude themselves into thinking, "Let me just do these other little things first. That way I'll be able to focus completely on the important thing because I won't have all this other stuff hanging over my head, so I'll really do a better job."

Good Stress/Bad Stress

When Sam said that he enjoyed the last-second approach that he was so used to, I understood fully what he meant. Like him—and, on more occasions than I care to admit, like me—procrastinators often wait to begin a task until they've run out of time, until they have painted themselves into that proverbial corner, literally creating the "high stakes" situation that their brains need.

Part of the problem for those of us with ADHD is that the attention system of our brain is often "sleepy" or lethargic when not fully aroused, so we go from stimulus to stimulus, from issue to issue, seeking ever immediate gratification and completely forgetting whatever it was that we were initially considering. We can't sustain the interest and effort and ability to focus on a single issue that, as adults, we're expected to have, so we're on to the next idea before completing the original one.

We're so easily lured into unrelated activities, in fact, that people suspect our motives, calling us irresponsible and lazy, undependable, and even self-centered. Well, some of us probably are, just as some people without ADHD are. We're human, after all, so we're subject to the same human flaws as everybody else. For years, we've also been told we're all those things, so some of us probably believe it, perpetuating the self-destructive myth even further. But for most of us, it's not irresponsibility or laziness or selfishness that lies at the root of our behavior. It's biology. And it's usually compounded by a lack of understanding about how to compensate for it.

"Stress Junkies"

We're called "stress junkies" with our need for high stimulation, but it's that very stress that actually focuses us. With it, we somehow prioritize better. We can suddenly sequence the steps we need to follow, and we can sustain the effort we need to complete the task at hand. We can stop "circling the airport," as one client put it, where "I see the target, I know that I'm circling, but I can't seem to land." With the right stress, we know that we *can* land, so we seek the stimulation that allows us to do what we must. Like anybody else, we like to feel good, and we choose reward over punishment every time. The problem comes when we feel good about the wrong things. Then the pleasure turns to pain when we realize we've disappointed those we love and failed to live up to our best intentions.

Although it sounds paradoxical, good stress and an aroused

attention system help us make the decisions that usually frustrate us into avoidance. When we can't imagine where to begin, we don't begin at all, doing everything else that we can think of to avoid the pain of being overwhelmed. Last-second stress turns us on, though, and in the frenzy of the rush, we can suddenly make the choices that paralyzed us earlier. How many term papers were written that way, how many exams passed, how many guest rooms and bathrooms and patios renovated for guests about to arrive? Being out of time has always forced people into action, but those of us with ADHD have a whole personal history to remind us how we get by.

I Know What You Mean

As a professional coach, I've been invited to give hundreds of speeches about adults with ADHD. Initially, I thought I could prepare for these formal addresses the way I did for informal talks during my Harvard years, when a few notes scribbled on napkins would get me through lunchtime talks to three or four professionals struggling with their ADHD symptoms.

When the first invitation of my professional career arrived in the mail, I was confident that I could do what I'd always done: Just before addressing the group, I'd madly fill a few pages with pertinent points, enough to hold the audience spellbound and make me feel proud of what I'd accomplished. In the rush and excitement of the moment, all the ideas would come tumbling out, and the most salient and poignant and inspiring stories—the ones impossible to choose earlier, the ones impossible to place in any order earlier—would be suddenly obvious to my fully aroused ADHD mind!

But facing an audience of hundreds, I immediately froze, and in the long thaw of embarrassment that followed, I resolved to spend as many months as necessary preparing for the next engagement, if any other invitation were even forthcoming. What I hadn't accounted for, of course, was the change in routine that my status as professional now demanded. I had deeper obligations now, and I would have to create new strategies to fulfill them—planning and gathering information and rehearsing—no matter how long and how painful that process might be.

Sam and my other clients had to learn the same lesson. What worked in the past needed to stay in the past. Circumstances had changed, and if they were going to gain the control of their lives they were seeking, they had to accept the fact that they were no longer college students whose only responsibility was completing assignments and passing classes. Now they had spouses and children who depended on them. They had bosses and partners and patients and clients to whom they were also responsible, and procrastinating was not an option.

N. NARROWING THE FOCUS

Breaking old habits is never easy. It takes time and persistence and resiliency to do things differently from the way you've always done them, especially when the old way was successful. Sam faced an even bigger obstacle, though. His procrastinating on one task was usually offset in his mind by the work he was doing on another, so he was confused about both Molly's feelings and his own. "I always *feel* busy," he told me. "It's not like I'm sitting around doing nothing. I don't get it why Molly complains. What does she think I'm doing?" Then he paused for a minute before adding, "I wonder what I *am* doing!"

Prioritizing Thoughts and Actions

The most difficult part of the A-N-S-W-E-R for Sam might have been narrowing the focus in the first place. Learning to prioritize his thoughts enough to know what to work on in coaching was hard work.

Procrastinators put things off because of the frustration of not knowing where to begin. Tasks and projects are circular in their minds, almost like the knights at King Arthur's Round Table, I often say, each knight as important and necessary as the next, none receiving more or less attention than the other. With that kind of thinking, it's impossible to keep track of priorities, since everything becomes as important as everything else. But before he could develop strategies for controlling his procrastination, Sam had to decide the areas needing greatest attention.

Doing Anything Else But . . .

In one of our earliest sessions, I asked Sam to recall, if he could, the events of the weekend leading to Molly's eruption. What was he doing when he wasn't working on the client presentation due the following Monday morning?

"There was other stuff, you know," he began, hoping perhaps that I'd accept a vague response and move on. Coaching wouldn't be helpful if it were that easy, I assured him, so I pressed on until he became specific. I also asked him to make a list as he spoke.

"Well, I knew I'd need extra computer paper," he said, "so I went to Staples early Saturday morning. I got a few pens there, too, and a lamp for my desk to replace the one that was all rusty. Molly hated it, but I told her not to replace it because I wanted to pick out my own. Sometimes I don't like . . ."

Then he paused, getting back to Saturday's activities. "The nursery Molly likes is about a mile from Staples, so I stopped there before I came home. Molly had been talking about wanting me to plant lilacs near the front porch, and, yeah, I remember surprising her with some. She really was surprised, too, because she thought I forgot about that, but anyway, I got the lilacs, but I forgot to buy peat moss, so I know I had to go out later to get some because after I dug the holes, I couldn't just leave them till the next day that way."

By the time the coaching session ended, Sam had a list

including Staples, the nursery, Home Depot, the gas station, the local hardware store, and an all-night convenience store for peroxide he needed when he cut his finger late Sunday while attempting to replace a cartridge in his printer. The list also included church, the bakery, the delicatessen, the local pizza store, a beverage outlet, and Home Depot yet again. "Oh, yeah," he remembered. "I went back to Home Depot again Sunday. I needed a new saw to get those branches down."

"Is there anything on the list that wasn't essential that weekend?" I asked. "Was there anything you didn't have to do while you weren't working on your presentation?"

Like so many procrastinators, Sam had been drawn into countless unrelated pursuits when he should have been doing what he'd been promising his partner for days. "Not to worry," he'd told Martin daily during the prior week. "I have all weekend free. I'll have plenty of time, so I'll do the whole thing then."

What Sam clearly saw was that he could have had the whole weekend free, but that despite his awareness of the need to get started on his client work—despite his intended goal—he had allowed himself to be busy with everything else. He was repeating the history with which he was so familiar and so comfortable, running from task to task in order to avoid a primary source of frustration, the goal he dreaded to begin.

"And why not run away from what you hate and straight toward what you like?" any procrastinator might ask. "Who would choose pain when there's pleasure to be had?"

The point, I reminded Sam, was to learn to derive pleasure from the appropriate source.

Self-Inhibiting

Sam needed to learn a new technique with which to confront procrastination, the art of self-inhibiting. He needed to screen out competing thoughts so he could focus on his primary goal, which meant that he couldn't let impulsive thoughts turn into self-defeating actions. Doing that also meant becoming more self-aware, not an easy task for someone who had taken self-deception to unprecedented heights. The list he drew up in our coaching session was step one.

Step two was turning such a list into a habit.

He could begin, I said, by writing down on Saturday and Sunday mornings a primary goal for each of those two days, followed just before bed by a list of what he actually did, similar to the one he had made for me.

Sam should have known, of course, that Molly didn't require the lilacs on the very weekend before his major presentation was due. He should have known that she could hate the lamp on his desk for one more week or even that, with no storm warnings in the foreseeable future, he could probably wait a few more days to remove branches.

Seeing in black and white where his time was going should make him more adept at self-inhibiting, I promised. Then, once he became aware of the things tempting him off course, he could begin to create strategies to address them. It would take effort to make the lists, and it might be even more difficult to look honestly at how he spent his time, but the reward of changing his life for the better would be worth it.

S. STRATEGIZING

One of the most striking things that came out of the early coaching session with Sam was his reaction to the list I asked him to make. He enjoyed recalling for me the weekend activities that preceded our initial meeting, and in their telling he was funny, reflective, and sincere. Of course everyone genuinely liked him, I thought.

He was also startled when he saw those activities in print. "I had no idea I got so much done," he said. "Too bad I couldn't have put all that time into what I was supposed to be doing."

Creating Accountability

"I hate asking anybody for help," Sam said. "Molly tells me it's a male thing, but I don't know. I'd just rather do things myself. She keeps saying, 'C'mon, Sam, why don't you let me, why don't you ask Martin.' I know it's because she really loves me and all, but . . ."

But being accountable to someone else has kept many of my clients on track, especially when they choose someone about whom they really care.

Because they enjoyed the comfort of shared history, Sam and Martin had always accepted each other's strengths as well as weaknesses, and they could dismiss qualities that others might criticize with "That's just who he is." They trusted each other implicitly, and Sam quickly saw the potential benefits of accountability. By revealing to Martin that he had ADHD, he could also ask Martin for help in accomplishing goals. Sam hated to disappoint his friend, and if Martin were privy to the goals he set, Sam believed he would try harder to accomplish them.

Creating a Competitive Edge

After opening up to Martin about his ADHD and his habit of procrastination, Sam asked his friend to serve as his accountability partner, someone with whom Sam could discuss both his goals and his progress in meeting them. Martin agreed to Sam's request, and in a "brilliant flash" a few months later—a throwback to their old teammate days, Sam said—Martin upped the ante in their partnership. What if they sat down each Friday after work and compared notes, he suggested. Whoever had completed less work that week would owe the other person dinner.

The minicompetition helped Sam to keep the most important accounts at the forefront of his mind and guaranteed he wouldn't procrastinate in beginning them. And as he continued to set manageable goals, establish timelines, and define milestones, he was creating a new habit along the way.

Chunking It Down

Like many of my clients who can see the forest but not the trees, Sam had trouble seeing the individual parts of major projects. In recognition of the difficulty he faced when tasks appeared daunting, he decided that he would try chunking—breaking down the large tasks into smaller ones and setting goals for completing each individual segment. For one thing, by creating more manageable goals, he was likely to feel good when he accomplished them. He readily admitted that most of his procrastinating stemmed from being overwhelmed when he faced the prospect of a major project. Smaller chunks of work would be more doable, and before he knew it, an entire project—a whole forest of individual trees—could be completed.

Chunking could also help Sam develop the new habit of success he needed to keep him focused on his primary goal. First of all, he would learn to accomplish important tasks without creating the last-second stress that had traditionally seen him through. And because he would be establishing specific, doable goals each day, he'd be cultivating another new habit as well.

Maximizing the Environment

Keeping their goals in mind has been a challenge for most of my clients. Listing what they want to accomplish is one thing. Seeing to it is another.

Sam continued to check in with Martin at work and with Molly at home—he had also asked Molly to help him be accountable—but he had to learn to track his own progress. First, he wrote his goals with big colored markers on a monthly calendar and posted it over his desk, where he could see it throughout the day.

Eventually, he learned to widen his perspective by posting a twelve-month calendar in his office at work and in the one at home. With colored markers, he mapped out the next twelve months of projects, with all the associated responsibilities and deadlines he could determine in advance. He created visual landmarks and accountability with Martin and Molly, and by talking out his actions and plans with them, he learned to keep his priorities in mind.

He used screen savers, too, reminding him, "Remember That Deadline!" and Post-it notes that he placed on the TV remotes and bathroom mirrors, even on the dashboard of his car. His environment became a virtual conscience, visual cues positioned like sentries around him to keep him on task!

Identifying Barriers

Sam discovered that keeping lists worked well for him, so he regularly reviewed his day with a list of what he'd done. What he saw were patterns of behavior, specifically the causes of his falling off course. He loved surprising Molly, for example, so he could find almost any excuse for being at the mall or at the downtown jewelry store or at the garden centers Molly was always visiting, and once there, he could find a hundred other things to grab his interest.

It was difficult to change that particular habit, but by seeing how often he'd made unplanned stops at Molly's favorite places, and by talking with her about it, he realized that he had been doing it more for himself than for her. "I know you like to surprise me, Sam," she told him one day, "so I never said anything before, but I think I'd rather be with you when you pick out things for me. I never told you before because I didn't want to hurt your feelings. What I really want is for you to keep focused the way you've been doing lately. That's the most important thing to me."

It took a while for Sam to process Molly's honesty, but in the end, he realized she wasn't being unkind or insensitive. She was being truthful, which they had both vowed to be if they were going to change their lives into something not just livable, but lovable.

Ultimately, it was Sam's lists that had propelled them to that point. He saw the kinds of things that lured him from his goals; now he could implement strategies to keep him on course.

W. WORKING THE PLAN

Sam could easily fall prey to his need for immediate gratification, and when the plan he had made faltered, as plans inevitably do, he had to be diligent and steadfast in pursuing it. He'd have to look at his visual cues, for example, and do what they said. He'd have to avoid those shopping centers and Home Depot aisles that enticed him, and he'd have to be honest about what he needed to do. No matter what, no matter when, Sam had to work the plan, stick to the plan, and not change the plan when he just didn't feel like doing it.

To convince him he wasn't alone in attacking what he'd normally choose to avoid, I told him about packing.

Years ago, I developed a ritual when it came to packing for trips, which had always driven me into such paralysis that I needed to begin the process at least two weeks in advance of any flight.

Up came the suitcase from the basement, and down it went in the middle of the bedroom floor, where I'd circle it daily, pretending that it wasn't sitting at attention like a prison guard, waiting. Days would pass, and still it stared, empty until the night before the trip—way into the night before the trip, actually, even until the wee hours of the morning, a few hours before I'd be taking off. I'd do everything else connected to being away, of course. I'd check the luggage locks, I'd label the keys, I'd label the work files I'd be taking along. I'd write notes—endless notes—to the dog sitter, I'd clip the dogs' toenails, I'd clip my own toenails.

Meanwhile, the questions would spin. What will the weather be? What mood will I be in? What will I want to wear? When will I exercise? Should I take shampoo or conditioner, neither, or both? Should I carry on a bag or check it in? But because I couldn't face the decisions the questions demanded, I delayed and delayed the frustration and pain of making them until the time came when I was out of time and I had no choice but to decide.

But until that last possible second, weighing all the options was overwhelming. I had to consider shoes, socks, hose, underwear, sweaters, skirts, slacks, toothbrush, makeup, hair products, computer. "Why don't I just take the whole house!" I'd scream to my husband. "It'll make my life easier!"

But I'm the coach, and because I can't preach without practicing, I couldn't just shrug and give up. I had to work and work at being able to pack, so I've managed to create a strategy that I—and my husband—can almost live with!

I still drag the suitcase from the basement two weeks early, but now, each time I pass, I drop into it one category of clothing—running clothes one day, dresses the next, robe after that—until at last everything's there. All I have to do the day before I leave is fold the clothes and arrange them neatly. I also keep a permanently packed toiletries case, complete with hair dryer and traveling iron, just in case, and I restock it the day after I return home. That way it's always ready to go, and I can just take it on the next trip, no decisions necessary.

The strategy probably sounds crazy, but it gets me where I need to go. Did I almost cancel a few trips rather than suffer through the agony that preceded them? Of course. But the point is, I didn't. I pushed through. I worked the plan, and I worked it again.

And the other point is this: The only way you can make progress and move forward is to keep working, the same way that I have to.

E. EVALUATING THE PLAN

Stuffing the suitcase while the driver honked in the driveway, dropping things I'd grabbed as I ran out the door, running back one last time for the forgotten cell phone—I knew there had to be a better way! And if I ever wanted to lose my dread of traveling, I had to devise one. My emotional well-being, not to mention my career, depended on it.

This evaluating phase of the **A-N-S-W-E-R** was just as necessary for Sam. It helped him slow down and take stock of his tendencies, and it also helped him realize his gains, especially when he began to derive satisfaction without the high stress on which he had usually relied.

He also discovered what didn't work. The auditory cues that so many other clients have chosen weren't effective for Sam. He had timers he never set, but he looked at his calendars all the time, so he realized that he responded best to visual cues and learned to strategize accordingly. The process of discovery is ongoing, so Sam had to endure the same trial-and-error process that we all do.

Mostly, he had to remember why he had come to coaching in the first place. He wanted to change. Sam had to take this evaluating step of the **A-N-S-W-E-R** to heart, even when doing so was frustrating.

R. REPEATING THE PLAN

Repeating the process might be the most difficult part of the **A-N-S-W-E-R** for you if procrastination is your primary ADHD challenge. You've spent years delaying the frustration of projects that overwhelm you, after all, and performing tasks and chores that, objectively speaking, were probably not a waste of time and that definitely were rewarding. In a different context, for example, Sam's planting of lilac bushes could have been fun and satisfying. It could have been received by Molly as an act of love, a way of beautifying their property, instead of as the source of tension that it became when it was done at the expense of a more important task.

If you're like many of my clients, it might be difficult for you to eliminate an old habit that, objectively speaking, appears just fine. Think of it this way: It's one thing to resolve never to engage in blatantly bad behavior, like lying to your spouse or using vulgar language with your child. It's objectively negative by any standards, so of course you should eliminate it.

It's quite another thing to understand why you shouldn't plant lilacs. They're pretty and they make you feel good and they can last for generations. Maintaining the resolve to change objectively benign behavior like that seems paradoxical. It means learning an entire new source of motivation and an entire new feeling of reward. It means learning a new habit and then re-learning it again and again.

But to reach the point of self-initiating changes and to progress beyond self-destructive patterns of behavior, you'll need to repeat, repeat, repeat the process that allows you to do just that. It's critical to remember that momentary successes never translate automatically into permanent gains and that ongoing success will be built on structuring, strategizing, and working the plan.

It's also important to stay focused on the big picture. Everything can seem interesting to procrastinators with ADHD, so you'll have to keep the right priorities in mind, updating your strategies to match your changing goals. Sam was fortunate, in a sense, because the lists that he enjoyed making kept him honest. He could see exactly what he had determined as his goal and then see exactly what he did or didn't do to achieve it.

The most common pitfall for any adult with ADHD is forgetting you have it, so, like Sam, you'll always have the challenge of remembering that your ADHD won't go away. Even as you celebrate your successes, you'll have to remember to pay attention each day.

It helps to have others in your corner cheering you on. "Molly and Martin have been great," Sam told me more than once. "Sometimes I just don't feel like sticking with the list and paying attention to schedules. I feel like just doing what I want to do, end of discussion! But then I look at them and I know how much

WITHIN THE BRAIN: THE ART OF PROCRASTINATION
by John J. Ratey, M.D.

Impaired executive functions in the frontal lobes, in particular erratic working memory and a faulty attention system, contribute to procrastination. Working memory can be likened to the RAM of a computer. Without sufficient RAM, the brain moves on to the next issue or stimuli, completely wiping clean what was being considered before.

Despite the awareness of the importance of getting started, the ability to procrastinate is often intertwined with the sometimes amazing ability of people with ADHD to forget, suppress, and repress their desired goals and "get busy" with some other activity, regardless of how meaningless it might be. Trapped in the moment, the person forgets even painfully catastrophic consequences paid in the past for their avoidance and procrastination. The double-edged sword of procrastination for persons with ADHD is that so often they are able to "pull it off at the nth hour." By activating cortisol, the body's stress response and stress hormone, dopamine, the primary neurotransmitter of the attention system, is released. This serves to correct the lethargic attention system and "turn on" the frontal cortex, which improves RAM and all the other executive functions. The person then is able to become focused and sustain the effort and attention to start and complete tasks. This is why individuals with ADHD develop the false belief that they will always be able "to pull it off." This works well until the complexity of their demands increases, and then they begin to fail.

they want me to succeed and I remember how much I want that, too. So I grit my teeth and dig in."

One way or another, you'll have to dig in, too!

Strategies for Procrastinators

You can try any of Sam's strategies as a start—*chunking, creating accountability partners, engineering the environment,* and *identifying barriers.*

Or try any of the following, again with your own touches added to suit your personal circumstances.

KEEP THE GOAL IN MIND

One of the hardest struggles for my clients is keeping their goals in mind. If you can't *see* your goals, you'll be more likely to get off track. Devise methods to keep the goal in mind and to see, and track, progress. Mark your goals, the way Sam did, with colored markers on a monthly calendar and post it where you will see it throughout the day, in the kitchen, perhaps, or over your workstation or desk.

CO-COACH YOUR WAY FORWARD

Find someone who has similar goals and work out a co-coaching relationship. Both of you, however, must be willing to do the following:

- Set up mutual goals and guidelines for the relationship.
- Be sure the co-coaching includes only what is appropriate. If it's about work, stick to work issues.
- Be consistent in your contact with your coaching partner.
- Be honest and open to suggestions, and trust your coaching partner to have your best interests in mind.

SEPARATE THE SETUP FROM THE TASK

Eliminate the confused feeling of "Where do I start?" by separating the setup from the actual task. For example, place a blank Word document with the title "Year-End Report" on your computer desktop, but don't start the report until later. You can do the same for paying bills by stamping and addressing envelopes at one time but writing the checks and mailing them later. Doing the setup as a separate task can make the task less daunting.

ESTABLISH AND MEET THE MINIMAL GOAL

Start by defining the smallest possible goal that will accomplish something meaningful on the project or task. Call this the "minimal" goal and schedule a time to complete it. At the scheduled time, do only what you stated as minimal, even if it's simply opening up a file and looking at the project for ten minutes. That's what I mean by minimal! This allows you to approach a tiny aspect of the project without becoming overwhelmed.

LIMIT TIME SPENT ON MAKING PLANS

Do you tend to spend hours making detailed plans with the best of intentions but never seem to get around to implementing them? Set a timer for ten minutes and allow yourself to write down only the basic things you need to do, not every single detail. Work on daily goals rather than scheduling every single minute. Then get moving!

USE REWARDS AS GOOD STRESS

Most of my clients work well under pressure, so try to use this insight in a positive way. Set a lunch or dinner date with a friend, or plan to go to a movie. Tell your friend you can't go until you've finished three hours of work on your project or until you've cleaned your house, for example, and say that if you don't finish, you *must* cancel. This is not meant to be a punitive exercise, but one to fire you up to get the work done.

CREATE FALSE DEADLINES

If you're avoiding starting a long-term project, find someone you respect (and fear a little!) and set several mini deadlines for handing in parts of the work. It can be your supervisor, your boss, or a trusted adviser. For example, tell the person, "I'll turn in a draft of the first part of the report by next week."

Many times, this "false deadline" can stimulate you enough to get the work done. This strategy needs to be used carefully because it's meant to create positive energy, not make you more stressed, so be realistic and don't overpromise!

USE A WITNESS

Clients often benefit from the mere presence of someone to help them start or complete a task. This seems to work well with tasks that have been put off for a long while or that are emotionally charged, such as doing the income taxes or clearing the house of clutter. Many of my clients don't need the person to help them with the actual task. Just making the appointment and having them show up to sit in the same room with them is enough.

USE A MODEL

If you are asked to write a report or do a project and are stuck, get a sample or a model to work from. This will help you see the end product so you'll know what is expected of you. It is a tangible way of having your goal in sight.

BEWARE PRODUCTIVE PROCRASTINATION

A majority of my clients fool themselves into thinking they're being productive by getting other projects of lesser importance off their plates first. Generally speaking, they can be incredibly productive doing everything *but* what they are supposed to be doing.

Beware! You are fooling yourself. Understand that much of this has to do with a sense of immediate gratification. See it for what it is. Use those small projects as rewards for actually working on your most immediate priority.

MATCH PEAK PERFORMANCE WITH PRIORITY PROJECTS

Do you know your "peak performance" time of day? When do you get the most work done? When are you the most focused?

Know whether you're a "morning," an "afternoon," or an "evening" person, and be sure to have your most important project in front of you at your best time. If you don't, you're apt to do a task of lesser importance and exhaust your energy that way. I've had clients who were morning people but who ended up regrouting their showers or balancing their checkbook during peak performance time. One devised a computer program that he wanted to market to banks, all the while putting his actual job in jeopardy.

YOU BECOME THE FIRST THING YOU DO IN THE MORNING

A well-known author and friend of mine once said to me, "You become the very first thing you do in the morning," meaning that if you do the thing that is most important to your career each morning, first thing, and if you make doing this a habit, you'll be successful.

Take this advice to heart, as I did. It has definitely worked for me in the writing of this book, and it has worked for many of my clients. It will work for you!

REMEMBER THE PAIN OF THE PAST

A typical pattern my clients fall into is saying to themselves, "Let me clear my desk of other work first, then carve out time over the weekend for project X," when history dictates that every time they do this, they put X off until the night before it's due. This tactic might have worked in high school, but you know it's not serving you anymore. Know that your brain will fool you in the moment and convince you that this time you'll actually accomplish it. Ask others around you to remind you of the pain of the past. It's one way you can stop this self-destructive cycle.

MAKE ACTIONS CONCRETE

Goals and plans are only wishes unless you establish a "when" for each individual step and action. Be specific on the breakdown of the steps you plan to take and the times you plan to do each one. Set a clear time and day for the completion of each.

ALWAYS HAVE A BACKUP PLAN

It's typical for my clients to sabotage their first set of plans and then to give up completely. Don't let that happen! When you mark out a schedule with start times and days to begin working on the project, set up several backup times so you can't escape starting work. For example, set a start time/day of Tuesday at 11:00 A.M. with a backup of Tuesday at 2:00 P.M., and then the *do-or-die* start time/day of Tuesday at 4:00 P.M.

SHARE YOUR GOALS!

Tell someone about your goals for the day. Sharing what you want to do helps in making it happen. Accountability can create the necessary motivation and help you to be more consistent.

CREATE "SAFE" HIGH STAKES FOR YOURSELF

This is a Nancy Ratey special. I used this strategy many times in the writing of this book, and I can say it really works!

People with ADHD often wait until they've boxed themselves into a corner before they finally start a project. I know this about myself, so I've used the knowledge to my advantage. I take my laptop computer and drive to a parking lot or to a park bench. I turn on my computer and basically play a game of chicken with myself. I sit there staring at the battery drain, and without fail, when it hits 73 percent, my brain kicks in and I start to write like a maniac until the battery drains. Then I head home. Doing this always guarantees me roughly two hours of writing!

UNDERSTAND WHY YOU CIRCLE THE AIRPORT

Some of my clients describe their tendency to avoid long-term projects as "circling the airport." They know what they need to do, and they understand the importance of starting, but they just can't seem to "land." What ensues is a cycle of self-loathing that perpetuates the "circling."

Understand what this is about. For some, it's an issue of not knowing where to start. For others, it's an issue of dreading what it will take to get the task completed—hours, if not days, of making up for having put it off. Simply knowing this can help you cut yourself off at the pass before you start to panic and circle again and again.

TAKE A PAGE FROM SAM'S BOOK

Sam's lists were his most important strategy, so they could work for you, too. Keep it simple in the beginning. Each day you're off from work, start the day by writing down your primary goal. At the end of the day, list as many things as you remember doing that day and put a check next to each one that was connected to your goal. It will give you a clear picture of the relationship of your goals to your actions. It will also show you the kinds of things that pull you off course, so you can learn to identify barriers.

It bears repeating that the only "best" strategies are the ones that work for you individually, so what is most effective will probably be what you create on your own. If something seems "almost there," modify it until it's exactly right in your own life.

And don't forget that trial and error will reveal what's best, which means don't give up!

CHAPTER 7

Impulsivity

Years ago, I was surprised when a client told me that during the twenty-odd years since he'd graduated from college, he had worked for eight different companies. "Yeah, I told my manager to shove it," was how he described the latest time he'd been fired. "And he told me good-bye. Too bad I'm so used to it."

Unfortunately, stories like his no longer surprise me. Many of my clients have gone from job to job, let go each time by employers no longer willing to overlook offensive actions and speech directed at clients, colleagues, and the bosses themselves. Sadly, these individuals have often been highly intelligent and skilled, in many ways so well suited for their jobs that success should have been automatic. What they've lacked has been a way to keep from saying and doing things so inappropriate that dismissal was their employers' only option.

When James, a relatively young client, told me a similar story, I knew that he was fortunate in at least one sense. He had only just turned thirty. Time was on his side, and with the right commitment and attitude, he could take control of his life.

One of the first things James said to me was, "If I could only keep my big mouth shut." He went on to paint a picture of a life beset by inappropriate behavior and mired in paradox. Young and independent, he was also handsome, athletic, and outgoing, a Wall Street trader on the fast track. He already owned a condo, a vacation club share in the Rockies, and a new sports car that he'd purchased for cash.

On the surface, he appeared rich and enviable and on the way up, the whole world within his grasp. He also loved his work, especially its intensity and pace, and though he'd been fired a few days previously, he was confident that he'd be back in another position soon. "That's not the problem," he assured me. "I know I'll get another job. I'm good at what I do, I really am. I swear I was probably responsible for about 40 percent of their accounts. I didn't get fired for bad work. I cursed at my boss in front of a lot of people again, and there was no way he was keeping me after that. I get it."

What he couldn't get was what made him act the way he did in the first place; why he said things that people found uncouth and offensive; why a former fraternity president and popular superjock couldn't keep a girlfriend for more than a few months while most of his old friends were settling down with spouses and children; why someone who'd already made "so much money that it's obscene" kept losing too much of it in casinos; why somebody who could make quick, lucrative trades on the floor of the stock market couldn't manage his own credit cards or save more than a few thousand dollars.

"What's up?" James wanted to know. "In the last two weeks, I lost my job, I got another notice from the condo association for parking in somebody else's spot, I sprained my ankle skiing, and Beth broke up with me. And, oh yeah, I forgot my mom's birthday on top of everything else, and now she's all hurt and mad at me."

Impulsivity

By his own admission, James was displaying some of the classic characteristics of ADHD, specifically an inability to control his impulsivity. "What's with people?" he asked, speaking about his social life. "What do they want, anyway? I see myself with a couple of kids someday, maybe a house at the beach, but, hey, I'm not ready to settle down yet. Women—they want you to check in every day, they want to know what you'll be doing six weeks from now, six years from now, and why don't you come meet their mother in Minnesota after you've only just met them. All these women in the city are so boring, they're all the same: Nobody just wants to do something without a million plans first, and it's like they want you to try out for some Mr. Perfect prize. Nobody knows how to have fun anymore."

Clearly, James was unable to understand that the frat boy behavior that had made him so popular in high school and college had worn thin. Old friends still included him when the Knicks or Jets or Mets were in town, but unable to predict what he might do or say next, especially after several drinks, few accompanied him on the ski vacations or fishing trips he often took, and no one invited him to gatherings including their wives and children. They weren't willing to take a chance on James when their families were involved.

Turned off by his excessive spending or rude remarks, newer acquaintances, especially women, were even less likely to last. At first he might seem charming and energetic and charismatic, but relationships usually ended abruptly when he was "loud, overbearing, and obnoxious, always the center of attention," a description Beth had recently invoked in ending their relationship. Other times, he simply got bored. The thrill of the hunt invigorated him, not the day-to-day commitment and empathy that invited intimacy.

Interestingly, this acting in the moment, quickly and immediately and without deliberation, served James well professionally, and his employers truly valued his ability to make instant trades and execute deals. At the same time, though, they considered him a professional risk, a constant liability who at any moment might lose his temper with a client or coworker. Trapped in the moment at any given time, he also regularly failed to complete paperwork required by industry standards, and his boss was sick of hearing James's excuses and empty promises to follow through.

"I hate all the rules," James said. "I don't even know what they are most of the time anyway, and if I do, I usually forget them at the wrong times because to tell you the truth, they bore me. Why do I need them, anyway? Everybody knows how good I am."

The A-N-S-W-E-R for James

Much of what James said in that initial interview troubled me, because I knew that if coaching were to make a difference for him, he would have to start assuming responsibility for his actions. At that point, everything was somebody else's fault: His friends were stick-in-the-muds, women were boring, his bosses had too many rules. According to James, he certainly wasn't the "real jerk" that Beth had called him. Everybody else was.

A. ACKNOWLEDGING THE ADHD

Probably the most important issue for James was acknowledging the reality that his problems would not go away by themselves and that it was going to take hard work on his part to change things. First of all, he had to admit several facts about his behavior: (1) He had an extreme attraction to instant gratification and high stimulation, regardless of consequences; (2) he never stopped to think before he acted or spoke; (3) he was constantly driven to increase the "intensity" in situations that were otherwise boring to him. Added to these problems were (4) an overreliance on intuition, and (5) an inability to learn from his mistakes.

Impulsivity was wreaking havoc with his life, and he needed to face up to the fact that he'd been deceiving himself. His quick wit had helped him succeed thus far, but he'd been equally dependent on adrenaline, a formula that couldn't last. He'd gotten as far as he could without a clearly identified long-term goal and a plan to achieve it. Now it was time to learn how ADHD was affecting his functioning and to take action to address it.

What Is Impulsivity?

Impulsivity is a lack of the brain's self-inhibiting function. In simpler terms, it's an emotional response to the world characteristic of childhood, rather than a rational response—one that includes deliberation, judgment, and reflection—characteristic of adulthood. Instead of thinking about their intended actions or weighing the consequences sure to follow, James and people like him leap before they look, with neither foresight nor hindsight to guide them.

Those who manifest impulsivity lack impulse control—a way for their minds to "put the brakes on." Without a cognitive response to a stimulus—without working memory or judgment or a way to evaluate consequences—they find it impossible not to speak their minds in the moment, and they often blurt things out, interrupt, or even finish other people's thoughts for them, eliciting a lot of resentment along the way.

True, it might be refreshing to hear somebody speak without a script once in a while, but it's also disconcerting to be on the receiving end of an unfiltered rant. Nobody likes it, and few adults are willing to put up with it. Nor are they willing to endure indefinitely the company of someone who constantly draws attention to him- or herself. To put it bluntly, that kind of behavior becomes embarrassing, if not exhausting, to be around.

Specifically, then, unless he began to understand what was causing his behavior, and until he created strategies to compensate for his impulsivity, James would continue to jeopardize any chance of acquiring new, long-term relationships of any kind. Whatever job he had at a given moment would also be in constant jeopardy, and money problems would continue to haunt him because of excessive spending and frequent gambling. If his impulsivity remained unaddressed, his struggles would be seen as character flaws or a lack of desire to change and improve. He definitely wanted to be married someday, but unless he took action to change his behavior, it was unlikely he'd ever find a lifelong mate.

In fact, James needed to understand that his neurobiology was at the root of his struggles. Acknowledging that his ADHD was causing—and, unchecked, would continue to cause—real problems was James's first step in understanding what he needed to do to help himself.

What Causes Impulsivity to Persist?

One of the most difficult struggles for people with ADHD is being stuck in the perpetual "now." James was unable to learn from past experiences in order to evaluate the potential consequences of present or future ones. Every situation was therefore something new, and his reactions were based solely on the moment in which he found himself. It's not unlike the person who continues to touch the lit burner on the stove, even though he's been burned every other time he's done the same thing. There's nothing in his head saying, *Hey, wait. Don't touch. You don't want to get burned again.*

Unable to remember that he'd already been fired from one position because of swearing at his boss, James repeated the same behavior, with the same results. It wasn't that he literally didn't remember his past actions. He knew full well that he'd been fired before, and he knew precisely why. But in the moment, as the new situation unfolded around him and his boss reprimanded him for not following company policy, his working memory of consequence failed, and he responded to that particular event with nothing from past experience to guide him: *You cursed at your boss before. You got fired for it.*

That's what happens to individuals with ADHD. In any given moment, they can't keep in mind the idea of the past or the idea of a future—that tomorrow or even an hour from now will actually exist. Mistakes don't get "cemented" in memory in the ADHD brain, so there is no plan in place to prevent new mistakes—mistakes just like the old ones—from happening yet again.

The same thing happened socially. Although James could recognize, after the fact, that he'd said or done something untoward or indecent or downright rude, he never had a lesson learned from the past to apply to the future. And because he had never learned to inhibit his impulses, no matter how many promises he made to himself or to others, he always forgot. A prisoner of impulsivity, he was truly a prisoner of the present, and a lonely one at that. The number of acquaintances he had used to be enough, he admitted. The quality of relationships was finally beginning to matter, and he wanted to acquire a few strong ones.

Intuition

Not too long ago, watching a family taking pictures with a throwaway camera at an important event, I volunteered to take a few with my own camera and send them a disk later. I don't know what moved me to step in that way, because I didn't stop to think about it first, wondering what they might say or do. I simply reacted to what I saw in the moment, a family obviously proud of the young man being honored. Perhaps the woman who accepted my offer was as impulsive as I, but that chance meeting has developed into a friendship I have no reason to think won't last.

One of the paradoxes of impulsivity is that, finely tuned, it can work to your advantage. You can read people and situations quickly and see things instantly that other people might completely overlook.

With its intrinsic pressure and intensity, trading was definitely the right line of work for James, no matter that he'd been fired twice already. His problem had nothing to do with his inability to handle the exhausting pace or make snap decisions.

The difficult challenge for James was nurturing the creative and beneficial aspects of his ADHD while compensating for its negative aspects—in other words, holding on to his strengths, even as he worked to rid himself of what led him into trouble. If he could remain outgoing rather than rude, and energetic rather than overbearing, then he'd be on the way to creating a fulfilling life. If, on the other hand, his intuition remained "untuned"—if it caused only more of the adverse behavior that resulted in losing both his job and his friends—then James would continue down a self-destructive path.

N. NARROWING THE FOCUS

Because he perpetually got himself into trouble by not remembering the consequences of past behaviors, James needed to identify a few things that happened repeatedly. He always chose instant gratification because he lost sight of the bigger picture. He was easily and frequently bored, so he created high-intensity moments, like gambling and clubbing. Friendships were important to him, but his desire to be liked led him into superficial relationships, where he had many new acquaintances but no true friends. People tired of him quickly, and they left rather than help him change or become accountable. He simply wasn't worth their time or emotional investment.

After listing those problems in his coaching notebook, James also listed long-term goals related to controlling his finances and impulse spending, as well as keeping his temper and language in check. He decided to begin by narrowing his focus to social skills in order to make and keep new friends. If he could manage not to drive people away, he could eventually concentrate on finding a true soul mate, someone with whom he could develop an intimate, lasting relationship—someone with whom he could build a life. "If I can learn to keep my big mouth shut," he said again, "maybe people will see I'm not really such a bad guy."

Adhering to Social Rules

Many people consider etiquette a quaint art of the past, but while no one can dispute that we seem to be living in an "anything goes" society, there is a breaking point. "Enough!" we eventually hear when someone has brazenly, or even inadvertently, crossed a certain line. "I don't have to listen to this, I don't have to accept this anymore."

Constructing a healthy social life would require James to adhere to social rules and to maintain personal boundaries—skills with which he, and most people with ADHD, generally struggle. Talking too much and interrupting others, for example, or being too "honest," without regard to anyone's feelings, is not acceptable. James would have to face the fact that even if talk show hosts and television personalities shout each other down with barbed insults and coarse language, ordinary people have a limited threshold for absorbing such insults on a personal level.

Most won't abide unreliability for too long, either. Repeatedly canceling appointments, showing up late, and forgetting important dates like anniversaries or birthdays test even a parent's infinite patience, and it's a rare individual—hardly a superficial acquaintance—who will put up with a pattern of it. True, James did not easily abide fools, but, just as true, most people do not abide constant rudeness. He needed to learn that behavior and respect cut both ways.

S. STRATEGIZING

To practice self-control over his impulsive behavior, James first needed to increase his self-awareness. Because he was usually unaware of his impulsive responses until it was too late, I asked him to try to isolate repeated patterns so that he could replace them with more appropriate actions. This would require planned, deliberate behavior, however, which was alien to his natural impulsivity, so I knew we'd have to proceed in baby steps to ward off his frustration. The first step would be to keep a log.

Creating Reliability with Himself

It was important for James to establish a sense of reliability with *himself* so that he could eventually become reliable in his work and social relationships with others. Many of my clients have found useful a motto I've posted in my office: **"I say what I will do and I will do what I say."**

Once James agreed to try implementing this philosophy into his own life, I asked him to identify and commit to one or two specific activities for each day, writing down only those things that must get done, as simple as locking the doors at night, for instance, or as necessary as mailing a birthday card to his mother. Once he was consistently accomplishing the items on the list, he could go on to phase two, monitoring his schedule.

Schedule Monitoring

I asked James to monitor himself every half hour over the upcoming weekend, a commitment that required vigilance and attention, neither of which came easily to his ADHD mind. Because he couldn't promise to keep his regular coaching notebook with him, he agreed to carry a small, less obvious pad, in which he had marked out his plan for each of the two days, everything he wanted or needed to do. Next to each, I asked him to write notations every half hour about where he was and what he was actually doing in relation to his plan.

What an eye-opener that exercise turned out to be for James! It didn't matter that a third cup of coffee hadn't been on his list, but a few other things were noteworthy, like the new ski boots he'd bought. The cost was not the issue, but the fact that he had strayed from his Saturday plan was. So were the missed phone call to his sister and the bills he hadn't mailed on Sunday afternoon. Both represented failure to follow through. "I say what I will do," he had promised. "I will do what I say." But it hadn't happened.

Over the course of our work together, James began to make small changes to address the impulsive behavior that he saw in his logs. He removed his credit cards from his wallet before he went out, for example, and carried just enough cash to cover necessities like lunch or dinner and emergencies like a flat tire or low gas tank. He deliberately stopped going to certain movie theaters to avoid the clubs he'd pass on the way.

Consequences

More important, he began to add to his logs the repercussions of his impulsive behavior so he could learn to evaluate the consequences of certain actions. Maybe he could excuse away an unreturned phone call to his sister, but he saw that it was a lot more difficult to dismiss his nephew's disappointment in its aftermath. Uncle James hadn't been there to see eight-year-old Jamie collect the soccer star award, not because he hadn't wanted to go, but because he hadn't returned the phone call to learn it was going to happen. Fed up by her brother's history of not responding to messages she'd left on his machine, his sister had refused to leave yet another reminder about the upcoming ceremony. "You're mean," Jamie had cried to James later. "Why did Mommy name me after *you*?"

Actions had consequences, James saw, and he admitted something for the first time. "Maybe Beth was right," he said. "It wasn't little Jamie who was being the jerk."

Asking For and Accepting Feedback

Working with me meant that James was accountable to me to follow up on strategies we designed for him, but he also needed to enlist the help of others when he was in the moment of impulsive behavior. If he could be aware as it was happening that he was interrupting, for example, rather than realizing it after the fact, he could begin to understand what he might do differently. The best choice of an accountability partner, of course, was someone he trusted and admired, someone with whom he felt motivated to change.

It's one thing to ask for help. It's quite another to be open to honest feedback, a second reason the choice of accountability partner was crucial. James had to keep in mind that he was hypersensitive to negative feedback, which he tended to regard as character assassination rather than constructive commentary. It was important that the person be able to use neutral, objective language ("When I was trying to answer your question, you cut me off before I had finished," for instance) and not sarcasm or criticism or judgment ("What's the matter with you? You're always cutting me off. You're so rude").

But it was just as important that James listen actively and openly to what was being said. Learning to ask for corrections is difficult, especially for high-flying performers used to orchestrating the moves, so none of what lay ahead was going to be easy.

Giving Others Permission

I know from experience that impulsivity sometimes makes me blurt out things that I don't mean to say, but even more, it makes it difficult for me to get to the point. I always do eventually, but in the meantime, I know people can get restless waiting to hear what I'm trying to say. Instead of taking the chance of losing them, I've learned to give them permission in advance to interrupt me with a leading question. "What point are you trying to make here?" they might ask, which immediately brings me back into focus. And it works as well for my listeners as it does for me. Instead of growing impatient as I talk and talk, they can comfortably and politely rein me in.

I suggested this strategy to James, as well as one that has worked for other impulsive clients—rehearsing.

Planning Ahead

Rehearsing is a way of planning possible details for an upcoming conversation so you can collect your thoughts ahead of time. It also helps you avoid emotionally charged, counterproductive responses to others, exactly the kind of behavior you're trying to eliminate. Keeping in mind the advice to try to talk about what interests the other person, James wrote several ideas in his notebook that he could use to rehearse for an upcoming date:

- What special interests does the person have?
- What things does the person enjoy doing on weekends or vacations?
- Where has the person traveled or lived?
- Does the person admire or look up to any particular individuals?

The idea was to practice focusing on the person he would be with, especially on keeping the conversation on the "higher ground"—nothing that should cause discomfort, but nothing blatantly superficial, either. Once he had decided on possible topics, he could then practice phrasing the questions the way he hoped to ask them, which would make them easier to remember:

- What do you like to do after work? What do you really enjoy just for yourself?
- What do you like doing on weekends?
- Where do you go on vacations?
- What kind of music do you relax to?
- Have you seen any good movies lately?

Rehearsing also meant considering topics involving himself, subjects he could talk about to uphold his end of the conversation. To help him clarify what he would say, and to make him comfortable talking about himself, I suggested to James that he write out answers to questions such as the following:

- What are the key things I want the person to know about me tonight?
- What interests can I talk about?
- What can I say about my job?
- What would be appropriate to say about my friends and family?
- What kind of language will be appropriate with a date?

People who are at ease socially might wonder about such deliberate planning ahead of time, but for James and those like him with ADHD issues, especially impulsivity, it can mean the difference between keeping and losing friends.

The strategy can work just as well professionally. Next time James had to meet with his boss, for instance, he'd be able to ask similar questions beforehand:

- What's the point of the meeting?
- What do I have to do to prepare myself?
- What language is appropriate for a business meeting, as opposed to a social setting?

Role-Playing

The bottom line for James was to do as much planning as possible to keep impulsivity at bay. Stressful situations had always triggered impulsively negative responses in him, so it was important to practice what he *could* say as well as what he *could not* say—and when he should say nothing at all.

Once again, James asked an accountability partner to help out, this time to engage in role-playing with him. Much to his surprise, his sister agreed to take the part of prospective dates, and because she knew him so well, she deliberately raised topics that would ordinarily cause him to erupt. In the beginning, he did erupt—he'd had a lifetime of practice, after all—but they kept rehearsing alternate responses until James learned to exert some self-control, at least enough to make another date possible. Two of his fraternity brothers assumed the role of either coworker or boss, and they and James rehearsed appropriate professional language and behavior, all the while testing each other's patience.

"I get so frustrated," James admitted as he recounted the early role-playing process. "I'm surprised they stick with me. Sometimes I say pretty awful stuff. I couldn't take it if it was me who had to put up with them."

W. WORKING THE PLAN

James's frustration was exactly why working the plan was so difficult, but it was also why it remained so critical. Strategizing and setting up structures hadn't been much of a challenge. He had enjoyed it, in fact, because he was by nature creative and imaginative, and he was always open to trying something new. But he was also easily bored, and sticking with an action, especially one that required slow, deliberate repetition, was uncomfortable and disconcerting.

James thrived on speed and intensity and high stakes. Recording what he was doing each half hour or thinking before speaking in his role-playing exercises was enough to make him run away from accountability. "I can't take this," he said too many times to count.

Creating a History

James had to create a method for keeping his future goals in mind. I suggested that he add to his logs a list of accomplishments and goals that he could review frequently, an especially important activity for someone who lives perpetually in the present. By studying his entries, James could begin to see the relationship between actions and results—causes and effects—and give himself something to draw on in future situations.

He could also see the impact of current choices on future goals, something he had traditionally been unable to do. Naturally, there were countless times when he became frustrated and impatient with the drudgery, as he called it, and with spending time on all that reviewing and figuring out and thinking about— all that *conscious thought* rather than the intuition and impulse on which he had long relied. As his coach, I cheered him on when he balked and stopped, and when he wasn't checking in with me, he turned to his trusted advisers and accountability partners.

E. EVALUATING

James wasn't kidding when he wondered how his sister and friends had maintained the patience and fortitude to stick with him. "I don't like being told what to do," he admitted, "and I don't want to hear what I'm doing wrong. If they start doing that, I wind up swearing at them or walking out of the room, and then we have to start all over. Who needs this?"

Many times he was ready to abandon the role-playing, abandon the accountability partners, abandon everything. And while it was obvious that he had to continue to create new strategies to

keep from getting bored, he also had to know the difference between ones that worked and ones that didn't and never would.
Role-playing was definitely working, bruised feelings and an occasional crushed ego notwithstanding.

Sign posting, on the other hand, didn't work. James had looked
at the sign in my office—the one about doing what I say and saying what I will do—because I drew his attention to it and talked
about it. And even though many of my clients use posters and
Post-it notes to stay on track, that strategy just wasn't right for
James. "I don't really like to read," he said. "It's enough to be
keeping those logs. I don't want to have to read anything else,
thanks. I don't care if it's only a couple of sentences."

It's natural and inevitable that clients discover their own strategies. Some will work, but others won't, and they'll know only by
evaluating what they're doing. For clients like James, whose main
issues are about impulsivity, evaluating anything is counterintu-
itive.

This part of the **A-N-S-W-E-R** process required more effort than
James had imagined. It took a while, but he did come to realize
that rehearsing and role-playing were worth the frustration they
often caused when he had to repeat the procedures after acting
or speaking inappropriately. He learned over time that he could
control his outbursts if he prepared for upcoming activities in advance.

R. REPEATING THE PROCESS

For James, easily bored and always searching for the next, more
intense high, the **A-N-S-W-E-R** process had to become a lifelong
reality check, the framework on which he would build the rest of
his life. Whatever phase of life he was in, he could rely on the
process for structure, which would be the antidote to impulsivity.

James had to incorporate the **A-N-S-W-E-R** process into his entire life, repeating it over and over again. By permanently keeping

a problem-solving log, he could learn to defuse emotions by distinguishing between the emotions themselves and the things that triggered them. To prevent potentially volatile situations from erupting, he could continue to rehearse appropriate responses beforehand. To clear his head of inevitable toxic thoughts before meetings or important conversations, he could call a willing friend and "rant" for a designated five minutes, and then go to the meeting, calm.

James had to remember two things: Self-management is a necessary life process. To counter impulsivity, so is the **A-N-S-W-E-R**.

WITHIN THE BRAIN: IMPULSIVITY
by John J. Ratey, M.D.

Impulsivity is one of the cardinal symptoms of ADHD and can lead to self-destructive behavior. What most people mean by impulsivity is that the person has to act immediately before thinking and considering consequences. It is often cited as a characteristic of immaturity in persons with ADHD and fits with what we know of the brain's development.

Until people are in their early twenties, their decision making and many of their responses to the world engage mainly the limbic area—the "emotional brain." We see little inhibition and little evaluation of consequences, or involvement of the frontal cortex. As they age, or mature psychologically, they begin to respond with the frontal cortex, or "rational brain," which helps to keep the emotional brain in check.

However, in individuals with ADHD, the rational brain is often slower to respond, which results in their having a quicker, more immediate reaction to the world. The limbic area overrides the prefrontal cortex, and thus these people fail to "think about" their response. Instead, they act.

Both coaching strategies and medication can help slow responses and "give a second to stop and think." Individuals with ADHD can also strengthen nerve pathways by practicing skills and strategies in delaying gratification and evaluating consequences.

Strategies for Controlling Impulsivity

Any of the strategies that worked for James might work for you, too, especially engaging an *accountability partner* with whom to *role-play* or *rehearse* before a social or business event. Since many clients have also found *keeping a log* and *asking for feedback* helpful, try those, too, as long as you're willing to accept the feedback openly.

Or try any of the following, being sure to give yourself enough time to evaluate how they're working. Change will not happen overnight, though, so don't give up after one or two attempts.

WRITE OUT YOUR SCHEDULE NIGHTLY

To successfully self-manage, it is imperative that you mark out a to-do list and a schedule at the end of each day. Waking up without a designated structure for the day is as good as taking a day off! Look at the schedule first thing in the morning. Make this a ritual.

CREATE A "HOME" FOR THOUGHTS

If you're someone who often complains that great ideas come to you in the middle of meetings or when you're concentrating on something else, you can capture those ideas by giving them a home and writing them down. Keep track of your ideas in a notebook or computer file so that you can get to them at a better time. The purpose is to provide "containers" for thoughts so that you don't impulsively act on them in the moment.

THINK BEFORE JUMPING

Before agreeing to work on yet one more project, join one more board, or meet someone for lunch, stop and ask yourself, before answering: "Is this reasonable?"

It is okay to say "no." Do not overextend yourself! Often people say "yes" too quickly without first thinking of the consequences. Have a dialogue rehearsed in your mind to be ready for requests on your time. Say, for example, "I need some time to think about how this will fit it into my schedule. Let me get back to you." If they demand an immediate answer, simply say no!

APPOINT A "WATCHDOG"

Enlist a trusted friend to watch over you and your actions. Give him or her permission to be very honest and to confront you if you are about to do something you might regret, like calling an old flame, for example, or walking off your job or skipping a business meeting. Go over a pre-agreed-upon dialogue for these circumstances—for example, "Jake, remember you told me to hold you back when you try to do these types of things because you forget the consequences." For this to work, you must allow the appointed person to become firm with you if you continue to try to justify your actions.

WHITE HOUSE DAMAGE CONTROL STRATEGY

One of my most impulsive clients surrounds herself with a strong team of advisers and uses them regularly. She says to build this philosophy into your life: "Don't make too many moves without consulting at least three trusted advisers. Choose people whose values are closest to yours and whose minds are more logical than yours." Using this strategy, you'll stay more on course by thinking through consequences.

RID YOURSELF OF TOXIC FEELINGS

If you do get sidetracked and consumed by toxic emotions, it's important to get rid of them before going into a meeting or having an important conversation. Do what James did. Call a (close) friend and say, "I have to clear my head, can I just talk at you? After five minutes tell me to hang up! Okay?" Then let it rip! This helps to clear your head of your extraneous thoughts and enables you to concentrate more fully on what is in front of you without the fear of blurting out something that you'll regret later.

LEARN TO SELF-OBSERVE

To help curb acting on impulsive thoughts, learn to "watch" yourself in action and monitor what you do and don't do. I personally pretend I have a minicamera attached to a hat I'm wearing. I try to observe myself through the lens of this camera—my hands, my body—in all actions I take throughout the day. I continually ask myself, "Am I on task? Off task? Am I where I am supposed to be? Am I working on priority items?" This strategy worked so well for me that once I slapped one of my hands when I noticed it had "wandered off" and was brushing my dog's teeth instead of remaining at the computer keyboard writing this book, where it was supposed to be!

DO IT ACTIVELY

Allow yourself to use flip charts or to hash things out on pieces of paper as you talk. Often, standing up or pacing while talking can help thoughts come together in a more organized manner.

BOTTOM-LINE IT

If you're like a lot of people with ADHD, you may have difficulty getting to the essence of a thought and will engage instead in long, descriptive stories. If this is you, practice the art of "bottom-lining," which means getting to the point. Ask yourself, "What is the key thing I want the other person to understand?" By clarifying your point this way first, you'll make it more easily when you actually speak to the other person.

Strategies for Developing a Social Life

In order to have a life outside of work, you have to have the ability to construct a social life. This means making and keeping a variety of friends, getting along with others in group situations as well as one-on-one, reading and adhering to social rules, and maintaining personal boundaries—skills with which people with ADHD generally struggle. Other issues can include talking too much and interrupting others, being too "honest," and being repeatedly unreliable with friends: canceling appointments, showing up late, forgetting important dates like anniversaries or birthdays. These symptoms often make you come across as arrogant, selfish, aggressive, or not honoring personal boundaries.

KNOW THE STEPS

The first step in knowing how to make and keep friends is knowing yourself. What are your interests? What types of things do you like to do? Once you can identify what your interests are, you can increase the opportunities of meeting like-minded people. That means locating clubs or activities that focus on those same interests. Next is carving out the time to be involved and showing up to meetings and activities so you can increase your possibilities of meeting people. Last, if you get nervous in new situations, you must have a dialogue rehearsed to break the ice and introduce yourself to others.

MAKE SOFT COMMITMENTS

Keep friends by keeping open the lines of communication. If you are the type of person who often backs out of plans because of overcommitments or gets overwhelmed at the last minute, simply let people know that you're making a "soft" commitment and not a "hard" one. Tell them, for example, that you'd like to go to the show and are tentatively saying yes, but that you might have a conflict and be unable to make it at the last minute. That way, you will avoid disappointing people if you don't show up. Do, however, have the courtesy to at least let the person know you're backing out as much in advance as possible.

PLAN! PLAN! PLAN!

If you don't make the time and space for meeting up with friends and having a social life, it won't happen. Learn to plan to see your friends and to have fun! Be sure to look at your calendar weekly and actually block out social time. Make a commitment and keep to it. Make it a regular and recurring activity so it becomes a ritual, like a movie on Sunday evening or a bike ride on Saturday afternoon.

KEEP ORGANIZED!

If you don't have or can't find your friends' e-mail addresses or telephone numbers, how can you keep in touch with them? Create a system to track these details. Put numbers in your Palm-Pilot or in Outlook, or type out a list and post it over your phone. Don't fool yourself into thinking that you'll find that Post-it note when the time comes and you really need it. Make creating and maintaining an organizational system for these details a priority!

THE SMALL THINGS COUNT

People with ADHD often let small things slide, like remembering a birthday, returning a call, or responding to e-mail. These small details can go a long, long way in helping to build relationships. Set reminders; write birthdays in your calendar or PDA, and make plans around the special events. If you don't have time to chat on the phone, at least acknowledge that you received the call and are busy, but don't just let things hang and expect people to understand. Making and keeping friends is a two-way street, and communication is a large part of it.

GET FEEDBACK

Some people with ADHD are very adept at social skills, while others are not. If you have challenges starting small talk or reading nonverbal social cues, for example, or if you simply want to improve your general social skills, ask a trusted observer for candid feedback on how you present yourself. This feedback can be invaluable in helping to know how you come across. It can help you learn to better self-observe, to fine-tune things like eye contact and table manners, and to avoid talking too much or too loudly.

DON'T LET YOURSELF GET TRAPPED

If you know you get bored quickly at parties, or get tired and want to leave but are dependent on others for a ride, plan an escape route. Drive separately, or take money for a cab. Tell your friends ahead of time that you might leave early so they're not surprised. Don't allow yourself to be in any open-ended situations if they cause you problems. It is essential that everything be as planned and structured as possible.

If you're trying to control your impulsivity, the key to success is to select a strategy, work through it, and judge its effectiveness. If you've given a strategy sufficient time and it's really not working, try something else.

Remember, impulsive people are usually creative people, so use that creativity to design strategies of your own.

CHAPTER 8

Distractibility

"I pulled a Lucy again," my friend Cathy joked the other day, a reference to the TV character of old whose antics constantly confounded her husband, Ricky, and who occasionally reminds us of ourselves. "I had another ADHD moment! I went to go out and I got in the car, I started it, forgot my list inside, and went back to the house to get it, the phone rang, I answered, and . . . well, you know the rest. An hour and a half later, I was looking for my purse and remembered it was in the car, and I went out and found the car still running in the driveway!"

And so it sometimes goes for those of us with ADHD, who find ourselves suddenly distracted from the task at hand and winding our way from one activity or idea to the next, "like somebody is clicking a remote control and switching the thought process in your mind," as one of my clients put it.

Cathy and I are lucky, though. We joke about what we sometimes do because we *can* joke. When we give in to distractions, we know how to pull ourselves back. We acknowledge our ADHD tendencies, and we're able to recognize when we wander off course. We're beyond the dysfunction that led to our respective diagnoses long ago, and we accept moments like Cathy's latest "adventure" as part of what living with ADHD means. We can laugh about things we do because (1) we already know we are *not* our ADHD—we've separated ourselves from this sporadic behavior; and (2) we have strategies and structures in place to keep us on track. Our occasional wanderings don't define us in our own or in other people's minds.

Distractibility

When they say they're distracted, most people mean that they're temporarily unable to focus or concentrate, a situational condition that will pass when the factors underlying it change. When individuals with ADHD are distracted, however, their condition is ongoing, a brain anomaly that leaves them unable to screen out competing stimuli or hold their focus on something long enough to do anything with it. Distractibility is a condition with which they live, a particularly troublesome one given a culture that appears bent on aggravating it.

Sometimes it seems that one would have to live out a vow of silence in a monastic cell somewhere not to be on sensory overload, scattered and frenzied and off in a million directions. As a people, we're wired and connected, clicking our way through the days, and for all the ways in which technology serves us, it also manages to keep us at its mercy. There's a constant demand from this technology-driven environment to shift attention quickly and often, to shift and shift again, so we have little time or impetus to think, let alone think deeply, about anything. The minute we try to focus on one thing, a light flashes or a ring tone sounds or a buzzer vibrates, and off we go to answer the call of what's next.

How to keep up? we wonder. How to *be* everywhere yet *feel* nowhere? So many devices, so little eye contact; so many rushed e-mails and voice mails, so little thought-provoking dialogue; so much noise, so little meditative silence. Who even knows what to do with quiet these days, except turn up the volume to drown out the discomfort of a solitary thought: "What am I missing?"

Most of us are stretched to the breaking point, with so many demands on our time and so many people wanting so many things from us that without the wires of interconnectedness, we fear we'll fall behind. And where will we be then? we wonder. Who'll get the edge if we turn down the volume and disconnect?

To one degree or another, everybody is rushed, everybody is scattered, everybody has those miles to go before sitting back and taking stock. The wonder is that somehow, despite their hectic and crazy lifestyles, most people manage to get on with the business of doing what they have to do and still remain in control of their lives.

Then again, most people aren't living with ADHD.

There's a difference in the degree and the frequency to which ADHD individuals are susceptible to all the distractions out there, and there's a major difference in the consequences of their behavior. They start off with a compromised ability to stay on task, and the demands of the click-click, push-button world make everything worse. "Oh, well, everybody feels this way" doesn't apply to them. Individuals with ADHD know full well that everybody does *not* feel out of control the way they do. What they don't know is what to do about it.

A Different Manifestation

While many clients jump from one activity to the next as a result of the distractions, others report an internal equivalent of all that physical movement, a hyperactivity of the brain. It's their minds that race, and they jump from thought to thought, from idea to idea. Paradoxically, they can appear "spaced out" when it happens, so they might be perceived as dull-witted rather than the whirlwinds of idea and imagination they really are.

It's especially disconcerting when their minds race during business meetings or while talking to others. Their attention wanders from what's being discussed to what's popping up in their own heads, so they don't listen actively to what other people are saying. Then, when they focus back in on the conversation or subject of the meeting, they're lost, which causes them great embarrassment.

"When I'm in a conversation with my boss or someone I want to impress," one client told me, "to make sure that I don't go off track every time a word triggers a new thought process, I have to tell myself over and over again to shut up and listen. It's like telling yourself to inhale and exhale. Usually after these conversations are finished, I have no idea what was said. I have an anxiety attack. I'm embarrassed and ashamed of myself because I have to end up calling the person and asking questions. Then the person is shocked that I was standing there and didn't listen. They end up thinking I'm stupid or dense."

It's difficult to explain to colleagues or friends that you zoned out for a while and have no idea what's just been said. It shakes their confidence in your intelligence, and they often suspect a lack of interest on your part when you can't concentrate enough to hear them. It's a lose-lose situation for both of you. The speaker feels devalued as a person by someone who they think won't pay attention and then becomes distant or even resentful in response to what he perceives as your lack of concern. Then you become defensive or withdrawn in response to that judgment, leaving both of you angry and upset.

"I wish I could explain how awful this is," that client went on. "I always feel so guilty when I've missed what my boss has said, as if I tried not to pay attention, like I did it deliberately. And then I get mad that I feel that way and mad at my boss for making me feel that way, even though I know he thinks he's the one who should be upset. Believe me, the whole thing stinks!"

Barbara—Dealing with Distraction

Barbara was a client dealing with distractibility. While preparing for a particularly important meeting one day, she found herself searching through piles of papers on her desk. As she was moving files around, she ran across parts of other projects that she'd been searching for earlier in the week, papers she thought she had lost, so she started working on those projects. "It was stupid," she said. "I had to meet a client at four that afternoon, and I should've been finishing the report for him."

It got worse, she said. "I don't know where the day went, but I went on the Internet to check something out for one of the projects and ended up spending the rest of the afternoon researching vacations. Before I knew it, it was three and I still had so much to do on the report. I barely made it to the client's office on time. I don't know how I got through the presentation at all. The thing is, it was good," she said, "but I'm sick of living like this."

That type of behavior was nothing new for her, after all. Like most of my distractible clients, she had a whole repertoire of stories like it. Not that long ago, she had missed a business meeting entirely, not because she'd planned to, but because she was following her unscripted thoughts. "I never mean to get sidetracked," she said by way of explanation. "All of a sudden I'm just caught up in something I never saw coming, and *bam!* Like that meeting—it's not like I was trying *not* to go."

But like so many other times, as Barbara was outlining the meeting in her head, something else had caught her eye. "I saw myself in the rearview mirror while I was driving over to the building," she said, "and I looked a mess, and I decided to make a quick stop at the hairdresser first, but then when I was having my hair blown out, I saw that my shirt looked all wrinkled, and when I went to get back in my car, I noticed a boutique somebody had told me about, so I decided to take a quick look for something else I could wear, and before I knew it I was buying a great new suit, and by the time I got to the meeting, nobody was there. They'd all gone already. I missed the whole thing."

A PATTERN AT WORK

Despite her erratic behavior, Barbara had moved up the ladder quickly at a major public relations firm, recently landing the title of executive vice president. Her innovative ideas had won over many clients and brought them wide visibility in some of the nation's most significant media markets, but although she was highly valued for her creative thinking, she was constantly struggling to complete projects and PR campaigns on time. Like other executives I've coached, she usually started out strong with the media campaigns she initiated, but once the initial excitement of creating something new wore off, she lost interest and lacked follow-through. Too often, the goal of completing a long-term project was too far off in the distance, and she failed to make the appropriate plans to reach it.

Working with her couldn't have been easy, either, Barbara conceded. She rarely returned phone calls promptly or sent e-mails when she was supposed to, and she frequently scheduled appointments that she ended up either breaking because she was unprepared or forgetting about entirely. "I know they think I'm undependable, I've heard them say that," she told me, "but they're wrong. Of course I get frustrated, I know I do, and I know I lose my temper," she added.

"I know the assistants all want to be transferred, because they say I blame them for not doing things I never even asked them to do in the first place," she also said. "But I really don't see that. They say I'm arrogant. I don't believe I'm the way they say. I'm not mean."

Because she often thought she'd told others what she wanted them to do, when in reality she never had, coworkers, and particularly her subordinates, could never understand what she expected of them. She was constantly changing plans midstream and coming up with new ideas. Details were frustrating for her to set out for others. They were in her head, which was enough for her. She couldn't understand why nobody else saw them the way she did.

Barbara wondered why so much was happening to her at this stage of her career. "I'm sinking," she said. "I'm losing my edge."

A PATTERN AT HOME

Because she had found it necessary to stay long hours after work to catch up on detailed paperwork and projects that had fallen through the cracks, her lack of organizational skills had also taken a toll on her personal life, almost driving her husband, Ed, out the door. "He said he's tired of seeing half-finished projects around the house, and he's fed up that I'm always staying late at the office," Barbara said. "But what does he want? We have a live-in, so it's not as if nobody's there for the kids. I try to do the shopping on the weekend, but he complains I end up buying a lot of junk food or whatever because I lose the list or forget to bring it with me. I just never get it right, he says."

Barbara complained that Ed treated her like a child. He was always calling her during the day to remind her of various things for home, or he would call if she had remembered to take her cell phone with her in the first place and then turned it on.

He had also started doing the things he wished she would do for herself, like putting notes by the door or on the seat of her car or even stuck directly to the dashboard. He had taken to commenting about the notes, too, she said, and commenting about how disappointed in her he had become, but despite his reminders and remarks, Barbara said she often forgot things anyway. "The nagging doesn't help," she said. "The truth is, it just gets me really annoyed when he thinks he's always right about everything, and then we wind up fighting."

What had happened to Barbara was exactly what I've seen happen with many of my clients. As her professional responsibilities increased, the challenges she faced were affecting her spouse and children, and the strengths she had used in the past were no longer sufficient to help her. When they were dating, and first married, Ed had seen Barbara's behavior as creative and spontaneous, and he had often remarked on her ability to think quickly and to breathe energy into even the dullest occasions. Now he viewed that same behavior as irresponsible and thoughtless, a source of constant strife, as he accused her of "not even caring" about him or their kids. "We obviously don't count that much or you'd do what you say," he sometimes told her. "We don't mean anything to you anymore."

Ed felt devalued, Barbara felt guilty and under attack, and both felt resentful, which are not uncommon reactions when one of the spouses has ADHD.

The A-N-S-W-E-R for Barbara

Like other executives with ADHD, Barbara had benefited from an ability to take risks, draw unique connections that others might have missed, and react quickly and effectively under high pressure. Her bright ideas and out-of-the-box thinking were rewarded in the corporate world, so her high-ranking executive status and the kudos she received in the field of public relations begged two questions: How could someone as successful as Barbara be seen as enthusiastic and committed on the one hand and arrogant and disappointing on the other? More important, what could she do to regain control of her life so she'd no longer believe she was *sinking*?

A. ACKNOWLEDGING THE ADHD

Barbara's first challenge was to acknowledge that she had ADHD. Only by understanding the neurobiology at the root of her behavior could she stop the self-blame, feel more in control, and create a plan of action. "I've been so depressed since I knew I had ADHD," she told me about her recent diagnosis, admitting that she'd done little to learn what she could do to compensate for her symptoms. She had merely felt sorry for herself, resigned to a fate she didn't think she deserved.

"To me it sounds like constant disorganization and forgetfulness," she said. "I didn't bargain for this, especially after I got the promotion. I thought everything would be great. Now that I know I have ADHD, I feel like I'll be a mess forever."

Distractibility as an Advantage

Interestingly, there can be advantages to the kind of diffused attention Barbara manifested. She was capable of seeing not only many facets to one problem, but myriad solutions as well. She could also see and pay attention to many things at once, while other people generally screened out competing stimuli and focused on primarily one thing at a time, shifting focus only as needed.

In her previous position as an account representative, Barbara had been responsible to clients for specific duties. When they needed to respond quickly to negative publicity or get the word out promptly about a new service or product, she was able to react immediately by hyperfocusing on the challenge at hand. In a moment's notice, her out-of-the-box thinking could turn negative publicity into positive action, and she could come up with original ways to present a client's activities to the public. By responding so well in those high-pressure situations, she had established herself as a jewel in the public relations field and was soon promoted to her current position.

Ironically, the same abilities that got her promoted were the ones that caused her trouble when her environment, and the demands it made on her, changed. In lower and midlevel positions, there is typically an established sense of structure over which an individual employee has little control. The inherent accountability and defined deadlines of such structure work well for many individuals with ADHD, so in her earlier, postcollege position at a smaller firm, as well as in her former position at the current firm, Barbara was in a perfect environment for someone with her skills and deficits.

For one thing, she worked closely with colleagues, who functioned together as a team, discussing projects out loud and interacting continually with one another. She worked closely with clients, too, where tasks were hands-on and the one-to-one interaction was stimulating. She always knew exactly to whom she was accountable for a project, and she was able to work with a passion and commitment noted not only by her superiors, but by competing firms as well. It was this energy, in fact, that had compelled her current firm to recruit her.

Distractibility as a Disadvantage

Being promoted had made life much more challenging for Barbara, as she faced the negative consequences of distractibility. She had been rewarded for success in the structured environment from which she had come, but she was now, paradoxically, held hostage to a lack of structure with increasing autonomy and flexibility, a potentially disastrous situation for someone with ADHD.

In this higher-level executive position, the onus had suddenly shifted from responsibility and accountability *to* others, to responsibility and accountability *for* others. She was expected to manage people, delegate responsibilities, write evaluations, keep detailed records, and hand in expense reports, all of which had to be self-initiated and none of which matched her strengths. She missed the order provided by her former superiors, an environment she was finding impossible to re-create for herself and those under her. Her department regularly appeared chaotic, with no one in charge of increasingly disgruntled workers. Barbara simply did not know what was needed, and because she was in charge, nobody else felt free to tell her.

Without the structure in which she had previously excelled, Barbara had no way to keep distractions at bay and fulfill the demands of her new position. The inability to rein in her attention meant that she often hyperfocused on one task to the exclusion of others in which she should have been engaged. When the stakes were high, that ability was advantageous, but since someone with a variable attention system cannot control it very well, especially if she's unaware that it even exists, she was often caught up in what struck her fancy at a given moment, something stimulating, perhaps, but simultaneously unnecessary, such as searching the Internet for possible vacation spots. Basically, she had no sense of priorities, and one activity was equally as consuming as the next.

Barbara's ADHD problems had always existed, but they became exacerbated by changes in her work status. Once she understood her ADHD, she could take responsibility for the symptoms that her new work environment had brought to light.

N. NARROWING THE FOCUS

Barbara needed a way to prioritize, and she needed a way to keep long-term goals in view. If she couldn't make the necessary changes in her department and in the way she conducted herself, she knew she couldn't last in her current position. But because she didn't possess an innate ability to do either, it was going to take concerted effort to set up systems and structures to address those challenges and to remember the need for constant vigilance.

In a way, the nature of her ADHD was the very impetus she needed to begin the journey ahead of her. By her own admission, she was out of time and out of choices. The stakes were high, so conditions were right for digging in and making necessary changes.

Lack of Planning and Prioritizing

What appears on the surface to be distraction for individuals with ADHD is often a lack of planning and prioritizing skills. When it comes to determining the level of importance of one task or activity over another, either they can't distinguish between them or they make the wrong choice.

It's not uncommon for people like Barbara to look at the piles of paper and folders in front of them and not know which one to attack first, not because they're trying to avoid the tasks, but because no one thing appears more or less important than the other. Barbara's need to look through old files, for example, seemed just as critical to her as her need to prepare the report for the client meeting later that afternoon. It wasn't that she was purposely putting off the report or that she dreaded doing it. She lacked the ability to judge the difference in importance in that moment.

On the other hand, when the choices are limited by a lack of time or when the stakes are high and immediate, people with ADHD have an uncanny ability to hyperfocus and choose correctly. They appear to be in complete control. Not only do they react well in the instant, they also prioritize the steps necessary to complete the task at hand, the very abilities that often elude them during less charged or calmer times.

Once she realized that she had little time left to do the report, for example, Barbara immediately assessed the situation as *Do the report or risk losing the client,* exactly the high-stakes, high-pressure moment in which she could excel. But it wasn't until she was under that extreme pressure that she knew she had to react. Her brain shifted into high gear, and the ideas flowed. Without that pressure, she'd been unable to make a choice of one project over another.

Inability to Focus on a Long-Term Goal

For adults with ADHD, a long-term goal is almost impossible to see in clear perspective. It seems too far off in the distance, like a mirage that comes and goes, so they shift their focus to something immediately in front of them with a more stimulating payoff in plain sight.

In her previous job, working directly with clients and having ongoing interactions with her team, Barbara was accountable for each of the many smaller tasks it took to complete any long-term project. Timelines were discussed and set up with the clients, and short-term deadlines had to be met on the way to completing the final projects. On her own, however, she had no idea how to proceed, so the long-term goal was never in focus.

It had been difficult for Barbara to admit at first, but by thinking about the specific effects of ADHD that she was trying to eliminate, she also saw that responsibility for compensating for her deficiencies was hers.

S. STRATEGIZING

So many of my clients have been derailed by distraction that I thought Barbara could benefit from strategies most of them had employed. Because one of her coaching goals was to develop planning and prioritizing skills, her strategies had to center on a sense of structure, the kind inherent in her earlier positions but missing in her executive status. She needed a new pattern that would help her become accountable to herself now that she no longer needed to report to managers on a regular basis.

A Master To-Do List and a To-Do List

I often recommend to clients like Barbara that they keep two to-do lists, one for the long term and one for the day. The long-term master list, which is especially helpful for planning long-term projects, includes everything you want to do over an extended period of time and is ongoing. It serves as a kind of long-term memory, allowing you to chart and accomplish short-term goals and eliminating worry about what you might forget over time.

The second list is for only those things to be done on a particular day. One possibility is to keep the daily list on a calendar, designed to let you see your goals as you're trying to meet them. Another option is to use a notepad with a fresh page for each day of the week.

Barbara had to commit to making her daily lists each day and every day. Not only would they remind her of what she planned to accomplish, they would also help her ward off distractions. The point of making the lists was to use them as a guide for her daily activities, and with a concrete reminder of what was important in front of her, she would be more likely to stay focused on her plan.

The daily lists had another function as well. By following them faithfully and crossing off each task as she completed it, she could develop a growing sense of what was important relative to what she wanted to accomplish. Had she looked at such a list the day she was trying to complete a report for her client, for example, it's fair to say that she'd have saved research about vacations for another time.

Considering Consequences

The critical step in learning about prioritizing came when Barbara added to her lists the consequence for failing to complete specific daily goals. It didn't matter so much if she forgot to pick up her jacket or skirt from the dry cleaner's, for example, because she had other clothes she could wear. It mattered significantly that she arrived at her daughter's spring concert during the last song, however, not only because while she was at her office answering e-mail, she had missed her daughter's solo, but also because she had forgotten the flowers the chorus would present to the director, disappointing everyone and embarrassing her child.

As Barbara realized at the concert, some actions, or lack of actions, carry deeper consequences than others. For individuals like her, who forget the importance of the long-term goal, ideas and tasks appear on a horizontal line of equal importance, not a vertical ladder of ascending importance. It was critical, therefore, that she find a way to establish the difference so that she could separate important concepts and projects from more trivial ones. Keeping a log of actions and consequences helped her measure the relative importance of items on her to-do list.

Visualize It!

To make your to-do list or calendar more real in your mind, sit down with it for fifteen minutes each morning and review what you've planned for the day. Study the list. Study the order in which you'll be doing things, and visualize yourself performing each item on the list in detail. Finally, do a "dry run" in your head. It might go something like this: Get in the car, drive to work, park the car, go to the office, place the to-do list on my desk, do *not* check e-mail, make two important phone calls . . . and so on. If you're a runner or if you go to the gym each morning before work, rehearse your day during one of those activities if that strategy suits your style. As long as the visualization becomes part of your early morning routine, it doesn't matter where you rehearse. What matters is that you do it.

End the Workday by Setting Up for the Next Workday

Because knowing where you're headed makes it easier to get there, and because it also provides a road map for where you are going—the structure you need if you have ADHD—I told Barbara not to leave the office without preparing for the next workday.

At the end of each workday, for example, give yourself up to thirty minutes to review your to-do list, seeing how many targets you actually hit that day. Make any necessary notations, look at your calendar to see what's scheduled for the next day, write your to-do list for that day, and then clear your desk as if you're finished working.

But don't leave! Stand up, stretch, then sit back down and pretend that you've just arrived at work the next morning. Look at your list and identify the project you're dreading most. Take out the necessary files or other items that you'll need to start that project and lay them on your desk as if you were going to begin working on them. Now you can go because your desk is set up to take on the project and you won't have to make a choice about what to do first the next day. You've already made it!

By setting up for each day in advance, Barbara would have an easier time initiating action, a skill she needed in her executive position. It would also improve her relationship with her subordinates. Being clear in her own mind what she needed done, she'd be more clear with them about her expectations.

Strategies for Focusing on a Long-Term Goal

You don't have to have ADHD to have a hard time focusing on a long-term goal. The end of a project can seem far off and the process of getting there insurmountable. It was easier for Barbara to lose focus and be distracted by—or actually attracted to—the quicker payoffs of completing projects on her daily to-do list. Shorter-term goals were easier to reach, and they didn't require the sustained attention that was so difficult for her. Their rewards were instant, exactly what her ADHD brain craved.

CHUNKING

Like many people with ADHD, Barbara was unable to break down large, long-term tasks into smaller, more easily achieved pieces, so she often avoided the big picture completely. By learning to divide a large project into chunks, however, she could move the focus away from the overall daunting task and direct it instead to discrete portions of the project, essentially treating each as its own task, with each carrying its own reward for completion.

She had difficulty initiating and returning phone calls to clients, for example. "I see a list of calls I'm supposed to make," she said, "and I freeze. I don't pick up the phone."

One solution was to divide the phone call list into segments and decide when they needed to be completed. She could use categories that made sense to her and that did not require prioritizing by importance, since she had yet to master that skill. If you have thirty calls to make, for example, you could start with those to your newest clients or to those first alphabetically, whatever basis you choose.

You're dividing the task into smaller, more manageable pieces, so you can also do as one of my former clients did and mark them off, or literally cut the paper on which the list is written into one section at a time, until you've made all the calls. That way, as the paper size shrinks in front of your eyes, you have a visual reminder of getting closer and closer to fulfilling the goal. Just remember that the focus should be on completing the project—in this case thirty phone calls—by a certain time.

BABY STEPS

Chunking is similar in concept to baby steps. Baby steps will help you avoid the feeling of shame that comes from not achieving a task that you were supposed to complete. They help you divide a long-term project into tiny segments spread out over a long period.

If the task is writing a report for an important client, for example, step number one could be allotting ten minutes to list the table of contents, followed by ten minutes to list the subjects that will go into the report. If you want to continue at that point, do so. If not, continue at another designated time.

The key to success with these interim baby steps is having a specific goal and a specific deadline. The important thing is holding up your commitment to each step along the way and accomplishing what you've committed to.

START AND STOP TIMES

Barbara said that she felt behind schedule much of the time and that many of the demands of her executive position left her feeling frazzled. "All these evaluations and records and expense reports—I can never get them done when I'm supposed to," she said. "Before I know it, I'm out of time, and whatever I was doing, well, that's it. I don't get to the next thing on the list, and then everything falls apart."

Most people with ADHD also report feeling behind schedule. They focus on one task to the exclusion of others, unaware that time is passing until there's no time left for the rest of the items that need their attention.

To make sure that she covered everything on her agenda, Barbara had to designate specific start and stop times for each item. If she were working on client files, for example, she could designate a ninety-minute period, stopping at the scheduled time to begin the next item, employee evaluations, perhaps.

It was the sense of being overwhelmed that had kept her from accomplishing even single tasks within her job description. Knowing that she would begin and end each at a certain time offered her a measure of control, not only over her day, but also over aspects of her job that typically overwhelmed her.

W. WORKING THE PLAN

Most of my clients are willing to try almost any strategy I suggest. The difficult part comes later, when they have to invest in the plan over the long haul, adjusting according to their unique strengths as they go along.

Barbara needed a way to become more aware of the passing of time, so after much frustration, she supplemented what she was already doing with her PDA. "I'm becoming totally dependent on it," she announced one day during a phone check-in. "I have alarms for everything, and for fifteen minutes before everything I have to do. I don't know what I would do without it. I can't rely on myself to look at my watch, so this is great."

She also thought that she needed more visual cues to help her stick with the plan, so she used a whiteboard in her office with outlines of upcoming plans to keep them front and center in her consciousness.

Mind Mapping

Mind maps can be used for anything that you're trying to put into order or into perspective. Essentially, using stick figures, pictures, or words, you brainstorm on unlined paper in pen or pencil, putting down all thoughts or issues that come to your mind at that moment. Next, you use colored markers to clump together similar thoughts or to draw arrows connecting related thoughts. If the ideas need to be broken down further, you can transfer the groups of similar thoughts to other individual pieces of paper, continuing in this way until you've seen each detail separately. You can do it by hand or use any of the many software programs that exist for this purpose.

Using an Administrative Assistant

Even with the many visual cues she'd engineered, Barbara was still floundering. Since it was clear to me that much of her earlier success had been predicated on accountability and teamwork, I suggested that she consider using an administrative assistant. She needed to work with someone who would be willing to handle her calendar, someone who would take seriously her need to be reminded—and rereminded—of meetings, deadlines, and projects, no matter how small.

"I'd be lost without my personal assistant," has been a common refrain among clients of mine who are plagued by distractibility. One client would have her secretary call her every thirty minutes starting two hours before she had to be at a meeting. Another, in order to take breaks during long meetings, would have his assistant page him so he could leave for ten minutes to take a walk and clear his head.

In addition to a personal assistant in whom she had implicit trust, Barbara needed to train subordinates to whom she could delegate responsibilities, people who would deliver frequent written and verbal reports on the status of projects. By surrounding herself with people who reported to her regularly, she'd be simulating the environment in which she had experienced previous success, one based on teamwork and accountability.

Obviously, it may not be possible to hire a new person to become your assistant, so you'll have to work with what *is* possible to effect the changes you need. I've trained my own assistants over a long period of time, and little things have made a big difference. I've told them, for example, not to let me keep the office door closed for more than fifteen minutes without checking to make sure I'm on task. The point is to be active in initiating the changes you seek, even if they seem like minor ones in the beginning. The cumulative effect of small changes will be a significant improvement in your ability to accomplish your goals.

E. EVALUATING

Being honest about progress during change is never easy for anybody, but Barbara couldn't afford not to be. She needed to understand how important it was to re-create the environment in which
she had been successful, one where she was responsible *to* someone, even as she fulfilled her responsibilities *for* others. Strategies to
self-manage were part of her plan to take control of her life, but she
also had to accept the role her assistant could play in managing her.

But because that could happen only if her relationship with
her new assistant, Rebecca, were truthful, open, and consistent,
she had to learn to accept feedback as honest observation, not
judgmental criticism. She also had to remember that, as difficult
as it might be to hear what Rebecca had to say, it would be just as
difficult for Rebecca to critique the boss, which was a reversal of
the natural order of things. Barbara would have to give her assistant permission and encouragement to observe her and rein her
in when she became distracted, not an easy thing when it's done
from a professionally subordinate position. She would have to be
as transparent as possible with Rebecca about what she needed
to accomplish at any given time.

The first thing her assistant said was that Barbara should work
with only one file on her desk at a time instead of the mass of
files that she always had. Each morning, Rebecca would come
into Barbara's office with only one set of files pertaining to one
project and then not give Barbara any other files until she had
completed the amount of work in the particular time segment
she'd allotted for that one project.

Rebecca also said that she was usually aware of Barbara's
deadlines, yet she would see Barbara doing other things that
didn't pertain to the project at hand. "I see you staring off into
space or sharpening a whole box of pencils or doing e-mails when
you're supposed to be working on a report," she told Barbara.

In response, Barbara asked Rebecca to point out such behavior each time she observed it. "But in the beginning that was really hard to take," Barbara admitted. "Who wants somebody pointing out everything you're doing wrong, even when you tell them to! I wanted to tell her to get lost sometimes, but she was really patient and consistent with me, which made it easier."

Many of my clients have created other strategies for staying productive. An especially helpful one for those who spend a lot of time in the office engaged in time-wasting activities is to pretend someone is watching you. By pretending there's a webcam or hidden camera in your office monitoring your every move, you eventually learn to self-monitor. Have in your mind's eye that your boss or your colleagues are watching you. It can make a big difference in keeping you on task!

WITHIN THE BRAIN: DISTRACTIBILITY
by John J. Ratey, M.D.

Persons with ADHD have a "sluggish" frontal cortex, which results in many of the manifestations of ADHD. Directly affecting focus is the ability of the frontal cortex to help block the entry or inhibit the entrance of other stimuli into our consciousness. If the frontal cortex is not working properly, the result is distractibility.

Also, owing to lowered amounts of dopamine in the synapse in the striatum, the reward and motivation area of the brain, the attention of individuals with ADHD doesn't remain motivated enough or fixed on a topic. It flips instead to the next new, and often random, stimulus that comes into awareness.

Increased dopamine helps rein in attention by making a particular stimulus more important. For example, rewarding, challenging, or intense thoughts or external stimuli can cause an increase in dopamine in the synapse, helping to increase focus and decrease distractibility. This is why medications such as Ritalin, which increase dopamine levels, are used to help correct attention issues such as distractibility.

R. REPEAT THE PROCESS

Barbara learned over time to alter strategies to suit new circumstances, and her vigilance and willingness to repeat the **A-N-S-W-E-R** process paid off. By engineering her environment to match her strengths, she was as successful as her superiors had predicted she would be when they promoted her in the first place.

Strategies for Those Derailed by Distraction

If you relate to Barbara, please know that just as she created strength-based strategies, so can you. I've had clients who write on their bathroom mirrors with dry-erase markers to remind them of their priorities for that week, and others who pretend to be taking notes during meetings to stay alert. Try any of the following, adapting them to your own needs and style.

FILTER OUT BACKGROUND NOISE TO ENHANCE FOCUS

Distractible individuals are overly responsive to both the external stimuli of their environment and the internal stimuli of their own thought processes. They act on the stimuli, jumping from thing to thing or thought to thought, captive to every whim and fancy.

Be honest about the kind of environment that suits you. To avoid getting carried away and lost, you might have to put yourself in a setting that is completely free of distractions—nothing on the walls, no music or ringing phones, total quiet.

FIND THE RIGHT PLACE THAT WORKS FOR YOU

If you know that working in a totally quiet space doesn't help you concentrate, then give yourself permission to go to a café or a coffee shop, someplace that has a bit of a "buzz" in the background. Many of my clients leave the office for a while and go to such a place to work on a particular project. They say that the "buzz" helps to activate their brain to screen out the background noise so they can focus.

USE MUSIC TO STAY ON TRACK

When I need to put in several hours of writing, I have one CD that I play over and over again. I use this particular CD only to write to. I've trained myself to sit down and start to work as soon as it begins playing. It took a while, but it works. Try it!

BE AWARE OF THE PASSING OF TIME

Wear a sports watch and set it to beep every hour on the hour to help you "hear the passing of time." When it beeps, stop and do a self-check. Ask yourself, "Am I doing what I am supposed to be doing?"

CREATE SELF-ACCOUNTABILITY EVERY HOUR ON THE HOUR

To make sure you stay on course and focus on what you need to be doing—and to learn to be accountable to yourself—take a Post-it note or a blank piece of paper and write down the three tasks you will complete over the next hour. At the end of the hour, throw away the piece of paper or Post-it note and write down your next three to-do items on a new sheet. These need to be concrete and doable, things like "Call Charlie" or "Water plants" or "Mail letter." Knowing that you have to complete the tasks within the designated time will keep you moving so that you don't hyper-focus on one activity to the exclusion of the others on your list.

PARK IT!

Whenever you get the urge to veer off course, park it. Designate a notebook or an electronic file for those extraneous thoughts that pop up. Get them out of your head and onto a piece of paper, delegate them to another time and day, and keep going.

This way, you *feel* as though you've acted on whatever it was, so it's out of your head and therefore out of your mind.

If you're someone who often complains that great ideas come to you in the middle of meetings or when you're concentrating on something else, you can capture those ideas by writing them down as they occur to you. This helps you gain more control over your creative ideas and your distracted mind, and it provides a way to follow up on your many great ideas.

MAKE IT A PERSONAL POLICY NOT TO MAKE STOPS EN ROUTE

Many of my clients, already on the verge of being late for a meeting or appointment, will decide to make a *quick* stop at a store or run a *quick* errand on the way. History, of course, will tell you the consequences of these actions: getting stressed, being even later, missing your appointment altogether, disappointing others, and beating yourself up for repeating the same mistake over and over again.

Post a sign on your dashboard that reads, "Don't Stop!" If you walk or use public transportation, stick a Post-it note on your wallet reminding you, "Go Directly to Work!" or, "Go Directly Home!" And do what it says!

AVOID THOSE TRAPS!

Don't fool yourself into thinking, "Oh, I can read one more e-mail before I leave for my appointment," or, "I can do X, Y, and Z really quickly before I go." Don't listen to that voice inside your head! It will only get you into trouble. "Just one more minute" doesn't give you more time; it only makes you late. If you know, for example, that e-mail distracts you, use a timer to signal you to turn off your computer an hour before your appointment.

BEWARE OF "SEE DO"

Most of my clients respond well to their immediate physical environment, meaning they get caught in what they call the "see do" cycle and forget their designated priorities. They answer each e-mail that comes in, for instance, or notice dry plants and begin watering, or look for a snack and start cleaning out the refrigerator.

If this describes you, set up visual cues to keep you on track. Post signs to yourself like "Complete project X by 5:00," or create a screen saver to scroll across your computer screen reading, "Where Is Project X?" For longer-term goals and follow-through, you might want to post a calendar over your desk or in your kitchen with the due dates marked clearly in neon colors.

NOW vs. NOT NOW

Ask yourself, "Does this have to be done by today?" If it doesn't, type or write it into your calendar with the date by which it needs to be done. Then you know that for now, it's dealt with. If you follow this process all the way through your list, you'll be left with only the things that must be completed now.

One of my clients uses this strategy to help him prioritize his to-do lists so that he's always working on the most important things on the list. He says it reduces his temptation to act on nonessential items, and best of all, it keeps him honest.

"If I have a long list to handle every day, I'm setting myself up for failure," he said. "I'm lying to myself. I've promised myself a million times that I'll finish the entire to-do list, but it's impossible. In the end, I look at all the undone items and feel demoralized . . . again. So I got rid of the lists, and it works for me, especially because nothing gets forgotten."

Maybe his strategy will work for you!

PREPARE AHEAD OF TIME

If you know you're frequently late to appointments because you get distracted, prepare as much as you can the day before the appointment. Put the files you need in your briefcase, the PowerPoint files on your computer desktop, your coat by the door, and so on.

Do anything you can to make it as easy as possible for you to simply grab what you need and run.

USE DISTRACTIONS AS REWARDS

Come up with a list of things you know will distract you, and use them as rewards. Plug in these items upon completion of a task or at the end of a designated time segment.

One client, for example, knew that computer games were definitely a distraction, so he scheduled playing a few into his work plan to keep him motivated. By saying, "If I work one hour on my report, I can spend ten minutes on computer games," he was able to complete his reports.

Do whatever fits! For this strategy, you have to ask yourself, "Is the reward motivating enough to keep me working at my assigned task no matter how hard it is for me to stick with it?" You also have to be very careful that you keep the reward time limited. If not, it will become a distraction again rather than a reward.

I've coached many clients like Barbara, and although it hasn't been easy, it really has been fun. The strategies that we've created might seem outrageous to other people, but I can say unequivocally that they've worked. Try your own, and be as creative as you want!

CHAPTER 9

Transitions

"I know what everybody thinks," William said in our initial conversation about coaching, "but they're clueless. Yeah, it's true," he conceded, "I probably look like I have it made—a great family, an unbelievable salary, the whole package. But nobody knows the half of it," he insisted, "the way I feel like I'm losing it half the time."

I could picture from his comments that William's office also appeared perfect, everything neat and organized and in its place, his files all labeled and in order. "I don't like messes," he said, "and I make sure everybody at the office knows to leave my stuff alone," which undoubtedly added to others' perception that here was a man in charge of his world.

As he indicated, though, it took a lot of energy to maintain that rigid aura of perfection, and he was feeling its weight. Things needed to change. The sense of failure, guilt, and overwhelming anxiety that William carried were too heavy a price to pay for the image he'd tried to project.

As a coach, I've heard versions of William's lament over and again from my clients, the disconnect between the way they're perceived and the way they feel, the overwhelming burden they carry of reconciling how they appear to others and how they feel about themselves. Each version of reality has its own set of expectations and judgments, and neither is easy to navigate for an adult with ADHD.

A Pattern at Work

In one sense, people had been correct in their observation about William's professional success. Unlike many of my clients, who find themselves distracted and impulsive and stretched all over the map, William had long exercised control over his own tiny universe, in which everything had its place and he knew he could function.

As he readily admitted, things at the office ran smoothly, thanks in no small measure to the decade-long relationship he shared with his assistant, Lynn, whose understanding of William's particular needs had deepened with each passing year. "I love work," he told me, "because I know I'm good at what I do. But without Lynn, who knows where I'd be," he added, acknowledging the crucial role Lynn continued to play in creating and maintaining the structures so necessary in William's world. "If anybody ever found out how dependent I am on her, they'd think I was such a loser," he said.

Before he'd hired Lynn, William had struggled to complete tasks, spending hours trying to wrap up projects and losing track of time in the process. Because he rarely blocked out sufficient time to prepare for upcoming meetings, he was constantly shuffling and rearranging papers at the last minute, racing out the door but arriving late anyway, frenzied and frazzled and stressed beyond imagination.

He had also been perceived as inaccessible, and he admitted to snapping at people when he was interrupted. "I'd get totally thrown, and it would sometimes take me hours to get back to what I was doing," he said about his earlier behavior at the office. "And it was always hard for me to let anybody else do things. I know how I want things done, and I couldn't stand it when they didn't do it my way. But Lynn gets me," he said. "She definitely does."

Although, as she'd told William on many occasions, she hadn't immediately understood his idiosyncrasies, ten years had given her deep insight into his need for regimentation and control. To keep him in balance, Lynn had gradually begun to make sure that each task, each part of his day, had been set up in advance so that he could move out of one task and into the next with sufficient time.

Lynn had also served as William's professional organizer and "keeper of the gate," taking responsibility to ward off the unexpected, any unanticipated interruption that could send him into a tailspin. "It's not all that easy for me to focus," he said, "so once I'm immersed in something, I can't stand distractions. Lynn makes sure nothing gets past her that'll make me lose my concentration. I'm amazed sometimes at how she doesn't need to be told anymore what I need her to do. She just does it."

Basically, Lynn had learned that William needed an established routine, so she made sure that telephone calls, morning and afternoon mail delivery, and meeting prenotification all occurred at specified times. Continual reminders were also necessary, so she established a color-coded calendar system of immediate, upcoming, and long-range meetings and projects. Over the years, Lynn had engineered the environment for William so that he could move from one task to another without being startled and stressed by an unwelcome change of plan.

The more Lynn understood and acted on behalf of William's needs, the more William had been willing to surrender to her the control over his environment that he desperately needed. It was a perfect working relationship: As Lynn took over control of the office, she gave back to William control over his day and time. He might have continued to appear to his coworkers as inflexible and obsessive about details, but his office was running smoothly and things got accomplished.

It wasn't what happened *at* the office that had prompted

William's call to me. It was what happened after he *left* the office.

A Pattern at Home

Many of my clients love the excitement of last-second deadlines and an unexpected turn of events. "It's that rush that gets me to produce, even if it does exact its pound of flesh from me and everybody around me," one client told me.

That's not how William functioned. He panicked at the unplanned and could do nothing. Because of his inflexibility, he and his family were suffering, but they didn't understand why.

"I really want to help Alene out," he said about his wife. "I want to be with the kids, I want to be a good father, but I can never seem to do anything right at home. I feel totally incompetent."

Before he even turned off the car, he said, Alene would be outside with a list: Take the kids to practice, pick up their friends on the way, stop at the deli. There was always something he hadn't expected, and it threw him every time. Even though he never meant it to happen, he and Alene ended up in screaming matches far too often.

Many of my clients have talked about similar behavior when they're caught off guard. They often lose their temper, even with their children, and then they feel guilty and remorseful for taking out their anxiety on people who don't deserve it. William knew he couldn't be as flexible as Alene wanted him to be, and he felt terrible that he was disappointing her.

Trouble with Transitions

Like many people with ADHD, William had always felt trapped in the present moment, making the transition from one activity to the next stressful and close to impossible unless it had been well planned. At the office, Lynn understood that he required a certain amount of time to find closure in one activity before moving on to the next, so she built adequate transition time into his daily routine. She also scheduled his meetings far enough apart that he could mentally withdraw from one before preparing for another, and she screened his phone calls and messages so she could give him a sense of order in going through them and in designating time to respond.

Nothing, in other words, was left to chance. As much as humanly possible, Lynn eliminated spontaneity from William's workday, building into his routine a multilayered system of structures that compensated for the difficulties with transitions that he experienced on his own.

But when he left the predictable environment of work, William arrived at the unpredictable environment of home, where chaos and kids are often synonymous. "I never know what I'll find when I get there," he repeated, embarrassed by the admission but agitated as well. He knew that Alene didn't understand how hard it was for him to function at home, and he was demoralized and frustrated.

Expectations

Transitioning from home to work was relatively easy for William because he knew what to expect when he got to the office. There were few surprises, so he didn't panic in anticipation of what might occur.

Coming from work to home was a different story. The only thing he believed he could count on was the *unexpected*. The anticipation of unscheduled activities, changes in plans, and altered routines was a trigger that set him off even before he arrived, and with no well of calm reserve on which to draw, he often erupted. Home was an environment he couldn't control.

Like other clients who have problems with transitions, William didn't know what to do. He didn't know what was expected of him. He panicked when he had to transition from his role as account manager, where he enjoyed success in an environment with set parameters, to his role as husband and father, where on any given day somebody needed something from him for which he hadn't been prepared.

The A-N-S-W-E-R for William

Connected as we are through technology to the whole world at once—or at least to a number of people at once—we have little choice but to shift on demand as buzzers sound and phones ring. Then we're forced to respond in kind, changing our focus and responsibility with each new call to become boss, assistant, spouse, parent, stepparent, coach, chauffeur, maid, tutor, and the host of other titles and job descriptions that make up a life these days.

"What a way to live," a new client said about problems moving from one role or task into another. "I swear, it used to take me so long to get into what I was doing that once I did, I didn't even want to stop for lunch," he said. "I was always afraid I wouldn't be able to get back into whatever I'd been doing once I started doing something else."

Transitioning often leaves those with ADHD not only unable to catch up, but also in a state of panic and/or paralysis.

A. ACKNOWLEDGING THE ADHD

People with ADHD tend to overrespond to stimuli. Those with transition problems interpret new stimuli as threats, which in turn causes the minipanics associated with ADHD. Almost any change can be unsettling and stressful—completing a task, taking a vacation, going from one appointment to the next, or receiving unexpected news. What they need is a way to change roles without anxiety and fear of freezing or exploding, even when those transitions have to be fast and immediate, coming without warning or time to plan.

The strengths and weaknesses with which William dealt at work could transfer into other environments, so he needed to replicate those conditions at home, even in the emotionally charged atmosphere of family life, where being detached and objective wasn't possible.

The fact is, William depended on structure and predictability, and when he feared losing the sense of control that structure afforded, he was constantly on edge. Coming home was fraught with anxiety, not only because of the potential for chaos, but also because he had a hard time admitting to his wife what he perceived as a weakness—his inability to handle spontaneous, unplanned activity. She, in turn, had little understanding of his need to know ahead of time what was expected, so the cycle of misunderstanding and resentment continued.

Professionally, William could execute plans successfully, but that was because of the strategies he and Lynn had devised. "Alene is always saying I don't pay attention to her and the kids the way I should," William said. "She doesn't understand why I can get things done at work but can't follow through with anything—*her words*—at home."

William acknowledged that in order to improve life at home, he would have to take control of his ADHD symptoms. One of the most important changes he had to make was communicating more with Alene so she could understand his need for structure and order. He also had to find a way to let go of the defensive responses that automatically surfaced when he felt threatened by the unforeseen.

N. NARROWING THE FOCUS

People with ADHD have trouble self-inhibiting. Even though they know intellectually that their overreactions don't make sense, they can be easily unsettled when they have to "reorganize" their brain and change focus. To initiate action to address the problem, and to let go of the self-judgment that leaves them feeling crippled and unworthy, they need to look at their struggles in one area through the same strategic lens they use elsewhere.

After exploring with me the conditions contributing to his professional success, William understood that his need to control was actually a strategic method used to meet his needs. He narrowed his focus to dealing with two specific areas at home:

- Communicating more effectively with Alene
- Transitioning from his professional role as boss to his family role as husband and father

Understanding and putting words to what he needed—communicating it—would be key to minimizing the chaos and ending the guilt and self-blame he felt when he couldn't meet his family's needs.

S. STRATEGIZING

In a misguided attempt to appear stronger than he really was, William had never acknowledged to his wife his specific needs and weaknesses. Rather than risk seeming weak or vulnerable, he had kept everything bottled up. Unfortunately, the frustration he then exhibited, the inevitable dysfunction in the face of the unexpected, appeared to Alene as controlling and rigid. If anything, William appeared willful and inflexible rather than anxious and out of control, as he actually felt.

Strategies for Communication

It was important for William to be open with Alene about his ADHD. He needed to tell her that he wanted to meet her needs and that he wasn't trying to be rigid and inflexible. But it was equally important that he communicate to her his difficulty shifting gears without warning so she could let him know, as far in advance as possible, exactly what she expected of him.

SCHEDULE TIME FOR TALKING

"It's really hard for people who don't have ADHD to know what it's like," one of my clients told me, which I know is true. It's easy to misconstrue erratic behavior and assign negative motives to what those with ADHD sometimes do, so perhaps Alene could be excused for wondering just what William's actions at home meant. On the other hand, William was *not* his ADHD, and it was important that both partners separate the person from the behavior, which could happen only through communication and hard work.

First they needed to set aside time for serious discussion—and if possible, the same time each week, so it would be scheduled—when the children were asleep or with a sitter and when there were no other pressing needs. That way, they could freely communicate their thoughts and feelings to each other without distractions. Many couples, believing that they already know everything they need to know about each other, resist such structured communication time, but when one of the partners has ADHD, it's not only important, it can also be marriage saving.

PARK IT!

Knowing that they had a scheduled time to talk about what was on their minds, William and Alene could then "park" the issues, especially the potentially loaded or toxic ones, until later. By writing them down for eventual discussion, they could be certain that the issues wouldn't be lost among the many other things that inevitably arose. They could also achieve a measure of distance and objectivity by waiting until a less emotional time, not unlike the old trick of counting to ten before sounding off.

The key was for both partners to be open and comfortable expressing what they were thinking and feeling. They also needed to be able to state their needs and challenges without interruption or blame, and they had to believe that they were in this together, neither one carrying a greater burden or compromising more than the other.

THINK IN TERMS OF THREE

To help eliminate blame and finger-pointing, I suggested to William that he and Alene try thinking beyond their individual selves to their existence as a couple, a discrete entity that needed to be nurtured every bit as much as each of them did separately. In a marriage, after all, one partner's problems never exist in a vacuum, and solutions for one are often new problems for the other. In their planned talks, William and Alene had to focus on strengthening the relationship, a third entity that they could work on together, shifting the problem and solution from either of them individually to what they held in common.

DATE NIGHT

William and Alene were not unlike many couples who completely lose touch with each other in the chaos of daily living. Interactions had become almost exclusively about house issues or the kids, and as William had implied, there was little intimacy left in their relationship.

But in order for intimacy to occur, there had to be a certain level of trust and safety between them. Communicating during their scheduled talks was an important step toward that trust, but it wasn't the only one.

Just as important was the need for romance and good old-fashioned courtship, which they could begin to recapture through planned dates, specific times that they set aside for fun as they used to when they were single. Anything that brought them together as a couple—dinner at a favorite restaurant, an evening walk after dinner at home, an overnight at an inn—was what mattered. Life hadn't always been about the mundane details and hassles of getting through the day, and they needed to remember what had brought them together in the first place. They also needed to express it, to say out loud what they loved and respected about each other.

As artificial as it may sound, that kind of planning and sticking to it is essential for people with ADHD, especially for someone like William, who needed to prepare in advance for what he'd be doing.

Strategies for Smoother Transitions

CHECKING IN

Because one of his goals in coaching was to establish ways to make transitions easier to handle, William began checking in with Alene as he was about to leave the office each day. By determining before he got home what he could expect when he arrived, he could plan for what was coming and even rehearse his actions and responses on the drive to his house.

WINDING DOWN

One of my clients leaves her office during lunchtime each day to eat at the nearby harbor. "If the weather is good, I sit on the lawn, and when it's not, I stay in the car," she said. "I just need to take some time by myself before I start the second half of my day."

To make the transition from work to home more gradual, and to buy him a little time between roles, I suggested that strategy to

William. He could take a short break on the way home, ten to fifteen minutes in a quiet place somewhere to relax and unwind
from the office. Even if he simply sat in his car for a little while
before starting the drive, the idea was to disconnect completely
from his work responsibilities so he could freely assume his home
responsibilities.

PLANNING TOGETHER AS A FAMILY

When I was growing up and living in different countries, one of
the ways my father kept our family structured was by posting a
huge calendar in a central location in the house. Each of us contributed ideas and noted responsibilities on it, and to this day, I
remember how important I felt to have even a small say in what
we were going to be doing.

I suggested a similar idea to William so he could see ahead of
time what was coming up in the children's schedules and plan
accordingly. The calendar would also give him a chance to establish backup plans for the inevitable changes in schedule that
would occur, and it would reinforce for Alene the importance of
letting William know as far in advance as possible if things were
not going to go as arranged.

By planning ahead for what to do just in case, Alene and
William could avoid the criticizing and finger-pointing that had
unfortunately become the norm. And as they worked together on
how to deal with unexpected changes, William could develop a
new habit of response when he was in a situation he hadn't antic-
ipated. Even the time to write the weekly schedule on the calendar could be planned—every Saturday morning or Monday night,
for instance, or whatever time everybody could be together.

Several months into coaching, William reported some success. "The kids needed to have ownership in the process instead
of having it imposed on them, so now they're learning some
structure, too," he said.

W. WORKING THE PLAN

William and Alene had to be very clear on their roles and expectations and very careful to keep their communication active and constant. No matter how productive any single conversation happened to be, they could not then dismiss the subject as settled.

Nor could they forget the importance of intimacy in their relationship. Couples have to take the time to foster intimacy. It doesn't just happen, and people with ADHD often don't slow down and consider things like vacations or time alone as part of what is needed to help their relationship thrive. If neither William nor Alene could handle details of reservations or vacation plans, then they could seek the services of a travel agent.

Finally, William had to accept the fact that his home environment would remain unpredictable. He was a husband and a father, and as such, he would always be dealing with the human dimension of those roles. The only thing that could, and would, change was how he would *function* in each role. It was up to him, with the help of Alene, to build into his day the time he needed to transition from businessman to family member.

And he had to keep at it, working the plan even when his enthusiasm for doing so had waned!

E. EVALUATING THE PLAN

"It's all about calmness," I heard from a client. "The calmer the transition, the more planned it is, then I'm fine. As soon as it gets to be a last minute scramble, then I'm crazy and more frustrated, but I have it figured out. I still tend to get pretty anxious about my ability to pull it all off, so I've learned to plan way in advance for handling family matters."

William borrowed from that client's approach. "Alene and I started writing things down," he said after a few months, "and it got much better. I don't feel so ambushed anymore. We got a notebook just for this, and she writes what she wants done instead of telling me all the time, and I check the book once a week and cross things off as I do them. Things stay calmer that way."

R. REPEATING THE PLAN

"Before I actually institutionalized the coaching plan into my life, I had much higher stress and wasn't nearly as resilient when the transition was necessary," a client told me as he reflected on his experience with coaching. "I realized that this was definitely not serving me or anybody around me, so it was a cumulative effect, and I realized that I had to do something. Once it was validated by reading all the material and educating myself about ADHD, I had to acknowledge it and work with it to the point where it wasn't an obstacle."

Like any behavioral shift, it takes effort, but once you realize how much better it makes your life, you'll know that it's been worth it. William worked hard at communicating his needs to his wife, and she helped build an environment at home where he didn't feel so out of control. Communicating was sometimes difficult for each of them, but they learned through trial and error just how important it was to William's functioning and their relationship.

Strategies for Those with Transition Troubles

Strategies for making smoother transitions focus on ways to lessen the panic by making the transition more gradual. Many of my clients have adapted the following strategies to their particular needs.

USE THE POWER OF VISUALIZATION

When making transitions, no matter how big or small, do "dry runs" in your head over and over again. Visualize every detail you

WITHIN THE BRAIN: TRANSITIONS
by John J. Ratey, M.D.

Evolutionarily, the startle response helps to protect us when we encounter new situations or ones that we perceive as threatening. Parts of our attention system are key in the startle: the amygdala and the frontal cortex. The amygdala, which I call "the intensity button," helps produce the response, and the frontal cortex inhibits and modulates it. When the amygdala is engaged, we startle and react by fight, flight, or fear.

In individuals with ADHD, the amygdala may be overreactive. The inhibitory abilities of the prefrontal cortex to still the amygdala and other emotional regions of the brain are less than optimal most of the time. This contributes to an overresponsiveness to stimuli with too much passion, too much emotion, or too much fear, quickly exciting the amygdala. The transition or change in the environment may be, and usually is, inconsequential, but the "startle" requires some reorganization on the part of the brain and shifting of focus. It can be very unsettling and cause an inner noisy state of high stress and anxiety.

This is when a minipanic ensues. Individuals with ADHD are thrown off track and into a new situation they interpret as filled with chaos. This causes them to feel lost and threatened. It disrupts their sense of context of their experience, and their anxiety in the situation is out of proportion. Without context, the discontinuity of the experience makes their anxiety worse.

can in making the transition. Sketch out times for ending each activity and starting the next. You need not follow the times exactly, but have an idea of when you will need to be switching gears. See yourself moving from one activity to the next.

LEARN TO LET GO

To transition successfully from one project to another, you need to learn to "let go" of the first and move on to the next. Many of my clients become perfectionists when it's time to move on to another project, and they find it hard to wrap up what they've been doing. If this is your tendency, set a specific stop time, then allow yourself fifteen more minutes and that's all. *No more!* You can always go back to the first project later, but the idea here is to keep moving forward.

DETAILED PLANNING

To have smoother transitions, you must be able to see beyond the moment. Sketch out detailed plans for at least three days at a time. This can help you (1) see more clearly what is coming up; and (2) identify priority items. Remove items from your schedule that can wait, and adjust accordingly when "unexpected" things crop up.

CREATE A "WIND-DOWN" ROUTINE FOR TRANSITIONS

This strategy is particularly useful for those who have assistants. Make an arrangement whereby your assistant will call you two hours before your appointed meeting, then an hour and a half before, and again an hour before, telling you each time exactly how long you have until the meeting.

If you don't have an assistant, use a stopwatch and set wind-down goals for each time juncture. For example, two hours before your meeting, start wrapping up whatever you're working on; an hour and a half before, prepare your files for the meeting; an hour before, finish everything you need for the meeting. If necessary, mark this plan out on paper with designated times and check off each step as it comes up.

THE ROLES BINDER

Use a three-section binder to ease the transition from one role to another, and label each section as one of your roles—"Social Worker," "Wife," "Mother," for example. Then list the daily activities for each role. As the last activity is completed, add notes to wrap up that role to put closure to it. Then open to the section for the upcoming role and look over the responsibilities and activities you listed. This will allow you to end one role and start mentally focusing on the new one.

WAIT TWENTY, THEN APPROACH

There is nothing worse for you and the people in your family than having a fight ensue five minutes after you walk in the door from work. Ask your spouse to give you twenty to thirty minutes after you've arrived home to "decompress." This eases the transition from work to family.

Strategies for Communication and Fostering a Relationship

LISTEN!

Don't assume that you know what your partner is thinking and jump to conclusions too fast. Try to listen actively to the other person's viewpoint. Breathe, take a minute, ask questions, and try to verify both your partner's feelings and your own.

MINIMIZE COMPETING STIMULI BEFORE TALKING

Does your mind wander when having a conversation with your significant other? Be sure to turn off the TV, your computer, or anything else that can distract you or take you away from the conversation. Have your partner ask you to maintain eye contact while talking. This way, you have a better a chance of staying focused on the situation at hand.

WALK AND TALK

If you have problems sitting and listening when your significant other is trying to talk to you, suggest that you take a walk while you talk. Movement helps keep the brain more alert and will help you stay more engaged.

COMMUNICATE IN NONTOXIC WAYS

Instead of screaming at each other, try speaking to each other in a calm and encouraging manner. Begin suggestions with "I need" or "I feel that," not phrases like "You don't" or "You always." Attempt to maintain eye contact when you're speaking to each other. This way, you both have a better chance of staying focused on the topic under discussion.

TAKE RESPONSIBILITY

Learn as much as you can about ADHD. Don't assign character flaws. Inconsistency in behavior, mood swings, and overpromising or underdelivering can lead to issues with trust. It's important to be able to explain the neurobiology of ADHD and realize that certain "traits" are directly connected to ADHD. Just be sure not to use ADHD as an excuse.

TIME-OUT

Effective communication also involves knowing when *not* to talk! There will be times when you and your spouse will have to recognize heightened tensions that exist between you and cut off the discussion. Agree to walk away for a few minutes to clear your heads.

BE THERE!

People with ADHD tend to get into an "all or nothing" mind frame and never get around to taking a break from work to have fun in their lives.

How often do you see your significant other? How present are you in his or her life? How can you expect to maintain a solid relationship with someone if you're never around?

If you make the effort to plan dates with your significant other, your relationship will be better for it. Have a travel agent book an annual trip for the two of you. Make it a ritual so you don't have to think about it. And don't even think about skipping it. Spending time together shouldn't be just a promise you make. It should be a reality.

DON'T LEAVE THEM WAITING

"Why can't you ever be on time? I told you about these reservations! Forget it. You're never here." Sound familiar? If it does, you need to analyze what it is that makes you late. For example, don't start working on a complicated project when you have only thirty minutes until your dinner date. Don't convince yourself that making that one call you have avoided all day will "just take a second." That "just one second" can lead to a very exasperated and hurt partner.

Strategies for Fostering Family Communication

MAKE IT A TEAM EFFORT!

No one lives in isolation in a family environment. Everyone's actions or lack of actions can have profound effects on the entire family unit. Make a family calendar of events, and involve everyone.

GIVE IT PERSONALITY!

Own that calendar by giving it your family's personality. Post it in a common area, and personalize it with photos and drawings as well as important upcoming dates, games, tests, and so on. Kids love having input and seeing that their activities are important to the whole family. They're also likely to assume more responsibility for themselves when they feel valued.

MEALTIME MOMENTS

Make weekend meals family specials by giving everyone a chance to share an accomplishment or a special event from the preceding or upcoming week. Talk about family plans, and initiate activities that everyone can engage in. Mealtime should not be for problem solving, so keep the conversation upbeat and positive!

Regardless of the challenges you're facing, it's important to recognize that those challenges have been, and will continue to be, ongoing. You'll need to be vigilant in telling yourself to stay on course, because no matter how many strategies you ultimately create, you can still be your own worst enemy, falling into the ADHD trap of forgetting the pain you've experienced in the past.

Without serious commitment to the **A-N-S-W-E-R** process, you can easily repeat, again and again, the negative cycles in which you've been trapped. Whether you select strategies for procrastination, impulsivity, or any of the other symptoms described in the previous chapters, you'll need to recognize the following:

1. No matter how subconscious it might have been, you probably did employ strategies in all facets of your life to get to where you are today.
2. These old strategies are no longer effective or sufficient.
3. You have to identify the triggers that lure you off course.
4. You need to identify your strengths.
5. You need to develop new strategies to handle your responsibilities.
6. Successful strategies are highly individualized, and finding them is a trial-and-error process.
7. You have to be vigilant and dedicated to make changes in your life.

PART III

Strategies for a Balanced Life

Now that you've read about coaching in general, and the **A-N-S-W-E-R** in particular, especially as it has applied to my clients, you've learned several things about living with ADHD. You know that ADHD is not a character flaw and that having it doesn't mean you're a failure, someone destined to disappoint yourself and others for the rest of your life. You can let go of that negative tape. You also know that ADHD is a neurobiological disorder that you can't simply wish away. But as my clients' stories illustrate, you can compensate for its effects. You can take charge and change the direction of your life.

If you have ADHD, you've probably recognized yourself in the symptoms and behaviors of the individuals about whom you've read. And even though, as a teaching tool, I chose to highlight only one ADHD symptom for each client, it's fair to say that I could probably have featured the same client in each chapter. Those of us with ADHD manifest many symptoms, so if you found yourself thinking, "Oh, that's me, I always lose track of time," when you read about Claire, and then, "Wait a minute, I have the same problems going from one setting to another," when you read about William, you're just like the rest of us. We're impulsive and we procrastinate and we're easily distracted, even as we hyperfocus and get bogged down in details. We're multifaceted, for sure, and we're multisymptomatic.

But we're also resourceful and creative, which is where coaching comes in. You've seen that structure is central to the tenets of coaching I've outlined for you, the single most important check on typical ADHD behavior. And you've learned that strategizing is the way to build structure in your life. Each strategy you create should be specifically designed to compensate for what your ADHD brain, unchecked, might lead you to do. You know that change will come from finding a way to use your strengths to work against your weaknesses. The point of coaching is to look objectively at what you want to change and then to create strategies that work for you, being as creative as you need to be.

Whether you hire a professional or decide to coach yourself, you know you have to commit to the process if you're going to make the changes you seek. You also have to be honest and resilient, and you have to be accountable. If you're like many of my clients, with a history of self-delusion and covering up, none of those qualities will come easily in the beginning, but a coach or trusted partner can help you develop them into new habits. It was true for me, and you've seen from my clients' stories that it can be true for you.

As you've also seen, there's no magic here. We who have ADHD struggle to keep our symptoms from controlling us, so let me repeat again: *We must create structure and strategies to compensate for our symptoms.* We learn from one another, we try out what has worked for somebody else, and we continue to experiment until we get it right. Then, because we continue to evolve, we adjust and try again.

Earlier in the book, I asked you to copy into your notebook or computer file the following table of ADHD symptoms and outcomes, but now I've added "ADHD Cause."

SYMPTOM	ADHD CAUSE	OUTCOME
Has a poor sense of time		Always late Accomplishes little Seen as undependable
Difficulty prioritizing		Often disappoints others Does work on wrong projects Avoids important tasks
Acting before thinking; getting bored easily		Spotty employment history Can't maintain relationships Can't tolerate boredom
Easily sidetracked from goal		Jumps from task to task Doesn't listen to others Misses deadlines
Inflexible; stuck in details		Can't let go Too controlling Easily agitated

Looking at the table now, you can probably guess why I originally left the ADHD causes blank. I wanted you to read about
my clients first so you'd have a context for understanding the
ADHD cause at the root of their behavior. With my clients' stories in mind, look at the completed table:

SYMPTOM	ADHD CAUSE	OUTCOME
Has a poor sense of time	**Time mismanagement**	Always late Accomplishes little Seen as undependable
Difficulty prioritizing	**Procrastination**	Often disappoints others Does work on wrong projects Avoids important tasks
Acting before thinking; getting bored easily	**Impulsivity**	Spotty employment history Can't maintain relationships Can't tolerate boredom
Easily sidetracked from goal	**Distractibility**	Jumps from task to task Doesn't listen to others Misses deadlines
Inflexible; stuck in details	**Trouble with transitions**	Can't let go Too controlling Easily agitated

To learn to self-initiate change and move forward, Claire, Sam, and the others had to separate themselves from their ADHD and know what was causing them to mismanage time or procrastinate or fall into any of the other ADHD traps wreaking havoc with their lives.

Now you know that you have the same obligation to yourself. You have to learn as much as you can about your own ADHD so that you can understand the cause of your behavior and separate yourself from what you do.

Earlier, I asked you to make a table of your own symptoms and outcomes in your coaching notebook. Go back to that table now and try to fill in the column marked "ADHD Cause."

Charting your own ADHD symptoms, causes, and outcomes is an important step in moving forward. Once you know what's causing the behavior you want to change, you can think about strategies to accomplish your goal.

While I was writing this book, I had the chance to reconnect with many former clients, all of whom generously offered comments and suggestions. "Strategies," I kept hearing. "Give as many as you can! We can definitely use them!"

In response to my clients' requests, I offer the next three chapters, each a compilation of strategies for aspects of balanced living that were not covered earlier. These strategies can serve as a guide to daily functioning, from getting through mundane, practical details of the day to enriching the spiritual side of who you are. I know that they work. I've talked about them at conferences and in various articles, and I've heard again and again that they make a difference for people coping with ADHD. If one doesn't work for you, try another. The key is to find something that will help you accomplish your goals, use it for as long as it works, and try something new when you need to.

All of this, remember, has one goal in mind. As I told you earlier, this is a book about possibility. May it help you take control, maintain control, and love the way you live.

CHAPTER 10

Strategies for the Home Environment

People with ADHD often live in chaotic environments. They misplace things, they jump from project to project randomly, and they leave things incomplete or undone. Lacking skills to prioritize, seeing everything as "equal," and not keeping things in short-term memory all contribute to making the tedious tasks of daily living—staying on top of finances, grocery shopping, laundry, or clutter—stifling. With the proper approach, these tasks can be managed and then mastered!

Finances

UNDERSTAND THE COST BENEFIT OF DELEGATING

If you're like most people with ADHD, you avoid details such as keeping up on bank accounts and paying bills on a regular basis. The thought of sitting down, sifting through mail, and writing checks is enough to make you run *from* the task, not *toward* it. Nonetheless, bills need to be paid or you'll continue to get late notices, accrue bad credit, or run the risk of getting your electricity turned off, not to mention upsetting others who depend on you. If this describes you, learn to delegate. Pay someone to keep track of your finances. Arrange for bills to be paid automatically via your bank. Do what you can to get the job done. In the end, it will cost you less than you're spending in late fees.

SEPARATE THE TASK FROM THE SETUP

To make paying bills easier and less painful, do the setup first before paying the bills, which is the real task. Equip a "bill-paying station" with your checkbook, stamps, envelopes, and a basket in which to collect the bills when they arrive in the mail. On a designated day, open the bills and stamp the return envelopes. On the next day, put your return address on the envelopes. On the next day, write and sign the checks. Then all you have to do is stuff the envelopes and send them! By separating the setup and execution, and by approaching the task step by step, you won't find it so overwhelming, and the job will get done.

CREATE ACCOUNTABILITY

I have several clients who meet with their accountant every three months simply to make sure they keep up with their finances. If this is something your accountant is willing to do, go for it! Your accountant can help you create systems for budgeting and tracking your income. Chances are, if left to your own devices, you'll get in trouble. Ask for help from an expert. You don't have to do it alone.

RITUALIZE IT

If you don't create space in your life for paying bills and reviewing finances, it will never come to fruition and will stay only a wish. Set a regular weekly time and place to pay bills and review your accounts. Mark it as an appointment with yourself and don't skip it, no matter what. Do it at the same time on the same day each week so it becomes a habit. Remember to choose a day when you are least likely to be distracted by a more entertaining activity.

STAY IN THE KNOW TO SAY *NO*

Stay on top of how much money you have in your accounts and how much you owe. For example, when you get your bank statement, highlight the amounts and post it on the back of your door so you see it every day. Lack of information about what funds are actually available to you at any given time is a recipe for spending beyond your means and ultimately for financial disaster.

CREATE VISUAL REMINDERS

Keep track of when bills are due. Post dates on your calendar. Or here is a favorite of one of my clients: "I open all the mail when it comes in and immediately sort out the bills, highlight the due dates, and tape them on the wall by the light switch. This way, I can quickly glance at the wall and know how many bills I have to pay and when they are due. Because they're right next to the light switch, I'm forced to look at them at least once a day!"

BUDGETING: CREATE A TRACKING SYSTEM

Keep track of receipts by labeling and carrying envelopes labeled "Business," "Groceries," and so on. Put receipts in the appropriate envelope when you pay for an item, and if you forget to get the receipt, write the cost of the item on the outside of the envelope. At the end of each month, file them away for your records in a small accordion-style three-by-twelve expanding file. This strategy is great for tracking receipts for expense reports, too.

Laundry
TAKE ACTION

People with ADHD are highly affected by their immediate environment. It's very important, therefore, to keep your living area organized and picked up. If you know you're challenged in keeping up with laundry, take measures to get it done. Either delegate it by hiring someone to do it or send it out to be done. Set a specific day of the week to do that, and write it on your calendar. Otherwise, the vicious cycle of having it pile up while you avoid it will continue. A messy environment also puts a strain on relationships and on those around you, so that's another reason to take action.

MAKE IT ROUTINE

You must create the time and space for laundry. Otherwise, doing it will remain only a wish. Set a time and day to do it on a regular basis. Think this out and make it realistic. Don't say you'll do it Sunday mornings if you go to church! That's setting yourself up for failure. If for some reason you can't do laundry on your designated laundry day, have a backup day and time. This way, it doesn't pile up and become unmanageable.

USE YOUR ENVIRONMENT

Planning to do it and doing it are two separate things. Be sure you have systems in place to remember the day and time you have scheduled. Post a note to yourself as a reminder, or put a sign over your laundry basket: "Do on Tuesday Evening." This strategy worked so well for one of my clients that when her fiancé saw the sign "Do Laundry on Wednesday," he thought it was directed to him and he did the laundry!

COMBINE IT WITH ANOTHER ACTIVITY

While you're doing your laundry, also do another project or task you engage in on a regular basis. This will help you to remember to do it more readily, regularly, and painlessly. For example, designate as laundry time Saturday mornings while reading the paper or Sunday evenings while watching your favorite TV show.

FOLLOW IT ALL THE WAY THROUGH

Doing laundry means folding it and putting it away, not just washing it. If you're going to take the time to wash it, take the extra five minutes to fold it and put it away. A pile of clothes on your floor is still a pile of clothes, clean or dirty!

Decluttering; Staying Organized

NO TIME FOR SHAME

The only way to truly overcome the "messy closet" syndrome is to come out of the closet! That means accepting that your struggles are not a character flaw. It's not you; it's your ADHD. This doesn't mean, however, that you don't have to take responsibility for doing something about it. In order to take that first step, you must acknowledge it's a problem and stop blaming yourself.

KNOW IT COULD BE EMOTIONAL

Going through old paperwork or clearing out clothes and clutter can be emotionally toxic, bringing up a host of feelings—shame, old memories, or horror that you've forgotten something important. Prepare yourself, and don't allow negative tapes to sidetrack you.

DOES IT HAVE A HOME?

Create "homes" for things like your keys, wallet, glasses, and cell phone—anything that you tend to lose track of easily. My husband uses a small basket in the kitchen as a collection point for these items. A client keeps a pair of glasses next to her computer, another on the bathroom vanity, a third pair on the kitchen counter, and a fourth in her purse. It's worth the expense, she says, to know she'll be able to read anywhere!

USE THE THREE-SECOND RULE

When clearing out piles of papers or clothes, or doing any type of decluttering, don't hold anything in your hand for more than three seconds. Make a quick decision: Throw away, take action, or keep. Cleaning can be overwhelming, so take frequent breaks, but continue the process until it has been completed. Set a time and day for each "take action" item, and *act* on it! For example, if you have a pile of clothing to donate to your local church, designate Saturday, 9:00 A.M., to deliver it.

STAND UP AND KEEP MOVING

Stand up while decluttering, especially while going through paperwork. Don't do it sitting down. Standing up helps your brain be more alert and prevents you from spacing out and/or hyperfocusing on one aspect of the job. Keep moving!

DON'T LOOK BACK

Once you've gone through clothes that you're going to give to Goodwill or decided on things in the house you're going to give away or throw out, *don't look back*. Put everything in boxes or in non-see-through garbage bags. Get them out of the house or stick them in the trunk of your car as soon as you can. Otherwise you might be tempted to go back through everything and keep things that you've already decided to eliminate.

DO A SWAP

Have a friend help you clean, and agree that, in return, you'll help him or her clear out clutter or go through paperwork. It's a lot easier having someone with you who can keep you moving and who has no emotional attachment to your "things."

KEEP IT ALIVE THROUGH ACCOUNTABILITY

The issue for people with ADHD isn't the lack of desire to stay organized; it's the ability to keep the importance of doing so in the forefront of their minds. Share your desired goals with someone, and keep him or her posted on your progress along the way. The power of verbalizing your intention, as well as having a watchdog of sorts, should help keep you on course and true to your plan.

IT'S A PROCESS—BE VIGILANT!

Remember that you have ADHD. It takes longer for you to change your old ways and develop new habits. You have to be committed to staying in for the long haul to make things stick. Don't give up! Discovering what systems and strategies work for you will take time. The worst thing you can do is give up. Know that you will slip and slide, but keep at it. It takes time to break old habits and develop new ones.

CREATE TANGIBLE ACCOUNTABILITY SYSTEMS FOR YOURSELF

Create time sheets for doing dreaded tasks. For example, if you need to clean out the pantry, post a piece of paper on the pantry door. On the paper list the task: "Clean Pantry!" Under that, state the goal for the amount of time: "Spend One Hour Cleaning Top Shelf!" The time spent can be spread throughout the day. It does not have to be done all at once. Every time you go into the kitchen, time yourself and write the time spent (ten minutes, fifteen minutes, twenty minutes, and so on) cleaning the pantry. When you reach one hour, stop. This serves two purposes: (1) to break the project into small, doable pieces; and (2) to allow you to actually *see* that you spent one hour's worth of time cleaning.

The key is to make your goal specific so that you can see and feel progress. For example, when you set out to clean one pantry shelf, you won't be able to miss the difference in how that shelf looks compared with the other messy ones you haven't yet touched. Or set out to do one load of laundry. You'll be able to see that the original pile has become smaller!

CHANGE SETTINGS TO GET MUNDANE TASKS DONE

If you can't do certain kinds of work in one room, try another. I find that I can't pay my bills anywhere except at my kitchen table. I have clients who take mundane paperwork and drive to a parking lot and do it in their car. Do whatever it takes to find out exactly what helps you focus long enough to get the task done!

CHAPTER 11

Strategies for Maintaining Physical Health

For individuals with ADHD, personal health is often a low priority. Lack of organizational skills and an inability to prioritize make it difficult to establish, implement, and maintain the necessary structures and routines to sustain good health habits over time. Things that seem simple for others—getting enough sleep, exercising and eating regularly, eating healthy foods, taking medications on a regular basis, and keeping up on personal hygiene—become monumental tasks for those with ADHD. Because staying healthy has a positive effect on everyone—especially those with ADHD—it needs to be a goal, and strategies for achieving and sustaining a healthy lifestyle need to be incorporated into your life.

Exercise

DO IT FOR YOUR BRAIN'S SAKE!

Knowing that exercise is good for your body is only half the story. Growing evidence shows the benefits of exercise to your brain. It's simply foolhardy *not* to exercise these days with the amount of stress we endure, with or without ADHD. Forget about looking good. Make your goal *feeling* good!

MAKE IT DOABLE

All too often we set ourselves up for failure with goals that are way out of reach. If your goal is to exercise for one hour a day, seven days a week, don't expect to fulfill that goal immediately. This "all or nothing" approach is a recipe for discouragement and failure. Be realistic and start slowly. The key is making the goal attainable and being able to do it on a regular basis.

SET A MINIMUM AND A MAXIMUM GOAL

Identify the absolute minimum you would require of yourself— say, jogging one time per week. Next, identify the most realistic number of times per week you *could* jog, a number that you could reach without too much stress—say, three times per week. Your exercise goal would then be jogging once a week, minimum, and three times a week, maximum. You'll most likely meet your minimal weekly goal or even exceed the maximum goal. What a great feeling it is to exceed your personal goal!

CREATE ACCOUNTABILITY THROUGH PARTNERSHIPS

If you know that working in partnership works for you and that doing things on your own doesn't, invest in a personal trainer. If you're unable to do that, find other means of accountability, like joining a running group or asking a friend who is a dedicated exerciser to join a class or gym with you. It's sometimes harder to disappoint others than it is to disappoint ourselves.

BE PREPARED AT ALL TIMES

If you tend to skip exercising because of forgetting your gym bag, keep an extra one packed with exercise gear in the car and at your office, one that is always ready to go when you are. A personal favorite of mine is to sleep in my (clean) exercise clothes. When I wake up, I can't escape remembering what I was going to do that morning—*exercise*. I have my clothes on and I'm ready to go!

KEEP A SCORECARD

Because the ADHD brain lives in the present, it's easy to forget past accomplishments, even if they're only a few days old. To combat this, make progress measurable by creating ways to track your progress. On the five days each week that he runs, for example, one of my clients writes on his calendar in black marker the number of miles he completes. Or you can use your calendar as a "scorecard." Mark an "E-Y" ("Exercise—Yes") on the days you exercise and an "E-N" ("Exercise—No") on the days you don't. The point is to see your progress and monitor whether or not you're reaching your weekly and monthly goals. Essentially, you're charting your own history of successes. The key is to make your tracking system visible and simple.

DON'T MAKE EXCUSES

Consider the time you have to exercise as an appointment with yourself, and do not break it! When you travel, call ahead and find out the hours of the hotel gym. Adopt a "no excuses" attitude. If you catch yourself negotiating with yourself about whether or not to exercise, stop and simply walk out the door to the gym. Even if you go for ten minutes, that's a win.

CREATE FLEXIBLE STRUCTURES

I use a system of "structured flexibility" when it comes to exercise. It's simple. I make sure I never miss more than two days in a row without exercising. I *must* go on that third day, no matter what. This guarantees me flexibility as well as exercising a minimum of two to three times per week without fail.

Sleep

IDENTIFY MEDICATION-RELATED SLEEP ISSUES

Some sleep issues may be beyond coaching and have to do with your medication. If you suspect that your sleep issues have to do with medication, please contact your doctor.

CREATE WIND-UP AND WIND-DOWN ROUTINES

Waking up on time hinges on going to bed on time and getting a good night's rest. Set routines to help you "wind up" in the morning and "wind down" at night. They can consist of anything from showering and watching the nightly news each night to having coffee and reading the paper each morning. The idea is to ritualize the routines you have created around getting up and going to bed.

WAKE UP AND GO TO BED AT SET TIMES

Establishing consistent times for sleeping and waking really works. Don't keep irregular hours, even on the weekends. Wake up and go to bed at the same time each day. This will increase the quality of your sleep by letting your body enter into a rhythm and help to destress you by knowing when your day starts and ends. Not everyone requires the same amount of sleep, but consistency is the key, so establish a routine and stick to it.

KNOW WHAT YOUR TRAPS ARE!

Problems with transitions can contribute to the struggle of going to bed and waking up. Because people with ADHD struggle with ending one activity and starting another, it's important for you to know your traps and be vigilant in avoiding them. If you know that talking on the phone, watching TV, or checking e-mail keeps you up past your bedtime, post signs reminding you to stick to your schedule. For example, don't allow yourself to go on the computer or answer the phone past 9:00 P.M. Ask for help from those around you so they know not to distract you from your goal. I had one client who knew he would sit and read for hours in his home office, losing track of time, so he bought light timers and set them to turn off all the lights in his office, jolting him into closing his book and going to bed!

SET A BEDTIME ALARM

Use a wristwatch with an alarm or set an alarm clock in your home to go off one hour before bedtime so you have time to get ready.

WAKING UP AND STAYING UP

Always have a backup system. Use three alarms if necessary! Set one in the bedroom, one in the bathroom, and one in the kitchen. If you turn off the one by your bed, you'll still have the other two ringing, forcing you to get up and turn them off. Or switch off with a friend, calling each other in the morning, and commit to it. The buddy system works.

Other strategies some of my clients use involve their senses: presetting their coffeemaker to go off so the aroma can reach them or purchasing alarm clocks with dawn lights that gradually fill the room with bright light. Some even sleep with their shades open so the morning light will wake them up.

Nutrition

UNDERSTAND THE BASICS

If you are not familiar with basic nutritional guidelines, take the time to meet with a nutritionist. Knowing the basic principles and food groups will be helpful when it comes to purchasing food, cooking, eating, and ordering food when eating out.

SCHEDULE IT OR IT WON'T HAPPEN

To have healthy eating habits, you must purchase groceries on a regular basis. This means putting grocery shopping in your schedule and sticking to it. Treat it as an appointment and don't miss it. Create rituals and routines to help develop a habit of grocery shopping.

MAKE GROCERY SHOPPING EASY: ORGANIZE BY CATEGORY

Most grocery stores are organized in food groups—fruit, vegetables, meats, cereals, toiletries, and so on. Create your shopping list accordingly. Organize your refrigerator and cupboards in the same manner so that you can see at a glance what you're running short on. Create a preprinted list of your usual items and add to it as needed.

MAKE IT A SOCIAL AFFAIR

Skipping meals defeats the goal of a balanced diet. If you know you tend to skip meals, make lunch and dinner dates with others you won't want to disappoint.

PLAN IN ADVANCE

Plan meals in advance. Have an idea of what you will be eating for each meal of the coming week. Having meals planned out will add structure and predictability to your week. Many clients will spend a day over the weekend precooking and freezing meals so they can defrost them easily during the week.

CARRY FOOD WITH YOU

I keep nuts, apples, oranges, crackers, and/or other health snacks in the car at all times. I have nuts at my desk and energy bars in my purse. This way, I don't get tempted to skip meals or stop and eat fast foods. The benefit is that my moods and blood sugar remain stable.

Medication

MEDICATIONS FOR ADHD
by John J. Ratey, M.D.

The best way to approach the issue of medication is to realize that some medications in some doses work sometimes in some patients, but not all of the time. The biggest problem in prescribing medication that will be effective for treating ADHD is getting the right dose and drug. With that said, effective medication depends on a good doctor-patient relationship, with open communication and good self-reporting from the patient to help home in on and discern the proper medication and its dose.

Generally speaking, the medications used to treat ADHD work primarily on the dopamine and norepinephrine neurotransmitters to help regulate the imbalances in the ADHD brain. Depending on the doctor's experience and preference, as well as on the symptoms of the patient, the doctor will make his or her best guess at the appropriate medication.

The major classes of medication to treat ADHD are the stimulants, whose actions are immediate, and the antidepressantlike drugs, which can take up to two to four weeks to effect a change in behavior.

MAJOR TYPES OF MEDICATIONS FOR ADHD

Stimulants:
Methylphenidate-type drugs: Concerta, Ritalin, Ritalin LA,
    Ritalin SR, Metadate, Methylphenidate, Daytrana patches
Amphetamine-type drug: Adderall, Adderall XR, Dexedrine,
    Dexedrine spansules, Vyvanse

Antidepressantlike action:
    Norpramin, Wellbutrin, Strattera

KNOW WHAT MEDICATION YOU TAKE AND WHY

It's your body! Know what medications you are taking and for what symptoms. Keeping track is the only way you'll know if they are working or not. Create a medication log targeting behaviors you want to change.

Keep in close contact with your doctor regarding side effects.

MEDICATION NAME:_____   **DOSE AMT:**_

SYMPTOM	DAY 1 RATING 1–3	DAY 2 RATING 1–3	DAY 3 RATING 1–3	DAY 4 RATING 1–3	DAY 5 RATING 1–3	DAY 6 RATING 1–3	DAY 7 RATING 1–3	SIDE EFFECTS
Lack of Focus								
Restlessness								
Impulsiveness								
Anger								
Distractibility								
Procrastination								

Rating Scale: 1 = not improved; 2 = improved; 3 = significantly improved

WATCH OUT FOR MEDICINAL SIDE EFFECTS

Many of the medications taken to treat ADHD can take away your appetite, so know the side effects of any medication you are taking. It's best to eat a little even if you're not hungry at normal mealtimes instead of skipping meals and bingeing when your medication wears off.

KEEP UP ON REFILLS

When you get prescriptions, mark on your calendar when the next refill is due, then work backward to the week the prescription is due. Set a daily reminder for every day of that week so you won't let refills lapse.

TAKE MEDICATION ON SCHEDULE

Do you tend to forget to take your meds? If so, don't fool around. Get a reminder system in place and use it. *Use your environment! Do what it takes!* Some of my clients use gadgets such as alarms to remind them, while others post notes on their bathroom mirror. One client rubber-bands his medication bottle to his toothpaste tube! Other clients keep their meds at their bedside with a bottle of water. The idea is to be aware of your tendency to forget and nip it in the bud with a creative strategy that works for you.

TAKE IT WITH YOU

Many of my clients keep small pill bottles containing their medications in their purse, car, desk, and kitchen cabinet. This way, they have their medication accessible to them when it's time to take a dose, so they're less likely to skip doses.

CHAPTER 12

Strategies for Maintaining Spiritual and Mental Wellness

Maintaining a healthy mental or spiritual life is contingent upon balancing work with play, taking time for yourself, and giving back to the community. Failure to adhere to personal boundaries, to keep emotions and negative tapes in check, and to curb impulsivity can contribute to diminished spiritual and mental wellness. When you give support to your internal life, your external life will also be better.

End the Shame and Blame!

The only way to stop blaming yourself for your ADHD is to learn as much as you can about it. If you can understand the neurobiological roots of ADHD, you will be better able to separate yourself from the disability and do something about it. The way to end the shame and start to build self-esteem and move forward is to make friends with your brain and develop strategies to bridge gaps in performance.

Make a Date with Yourself

Block out "sacred time" weekly to rejuvenate. Don't allow *anything* to creep into this space. For example, if you've decided to use this time to read and relax, don't allow yourself to clean your house instead because you have a day off. To help put boundaries around this sacred space, make a list of what is permitted in that space and time and what is not. Post it! Review it, and practice sticking to it!

Hold Yourself Back! Learn to Say "No"!

Learn to say "no." The word *yes* flies out of our mouths way too often, and we end up overcommitting and stretching ourselves way too thin. Each day, say "no" to something, no matter how big or small, so you get comfortable saying it. Create a variety of dialogues that will help you hold yourself back from various situations. For instance, if your friend or colleague asks you to make plans for the upcoming weekend, say, "I'd like to give this some more thought before I commit. Can you check back with me tomorrow?"

When You Say "Yes," You Also Mean "No"

Often, we don't think of the consequences of saying "yes." Stop and think before committing. When you say "yes" to something, what are you saying "no" to? For example, if you say "yes" to doing an extra project at work or helping a friend move on a Saturday, are you saying "no" to spending more time with your family or to taking time to exercise? What are you saying "yes" to in your life? What are you saying "no" to? What is it costing you? Try to ensure that "yes" adds something to your life.

Keep Perspective—Be Comfortable in the Gray Zone

In times of crisis or stress, your sense of clarity can be skewed and the desire to make things "black or white" can be very compelling. Be sure to be flexible with yourself and others. Allow yourself time to be in the "gray zone," especially if there is a crisis that is out of your control, like a death or divorce. Recovery can't be forced, so let your emotion run its course. In time, the fog will lift, and your energy and clarity will return.

Journal Your Emotions

If you frequently deal with "runaway emotions" or "negative tapes," you probably get locked onto thoughts or issues, unable to let go. By keeping a problem-solving log, you can defuse emotions by distinguishing what they are and what they are associated with. Write in the log whenever your emotions are preventing you from moving forward. The log can lead you through a series of questions that you ask yourself, such as, "What specific situation triggered my sadness?" "What specific action did I take in the situation?" "What could I have done differently?" "What specific action can I take now?" Answering questions like these can help you step back, see the issue in perspective, and recognize that you have the power to deal with it. This helps you let go of the feelings you are overwhelmed by, gain a new perspective, and move on.

Plan in Advance for Potential Emotional Upheavals

To help prevent or minimize emotional upheavals, make detailed plans for any times you find potentially volatile, such as holidays or unstructured time. Write out or go over dialogues in your head of what you will say in particular situations and how you will say it. Have an "escape" plan. For example, I have a client who gets in her car and goes to sit in a parking lot for a little while to take a break from the traditional Christmas Day celebration with her extended family each year. She returns renewed and more able to participate in the holiday festivities.

Create a History and Future for Yourself

Keep a journal of past accomplishments, future goals, and plans. Review it regularly. Typically, individuals with ADHD live in the moment, which lends itself to a host of problems: not thinking of consequences before acting on thoughts; forgetting past accomplishments as well as past failures; not thinking of the impact of current choices on a future goal, even a short-term one. The feeling of being perpetually trapped in the present can often lead to feelings of emptiness and lack of direction. Having a list of past accomplishments can help to shift your focus to the success you've already achieved. It can also encourage you to believe that you can succeed again and achieve what you set out to do.

Beware Letdowns After Completing Big Projects or Accomplishments

Many of my clients immediately go into a depression after they complete a large project. All of a sudden the pressure is off, and nothing seems "exciting" or relevant. Know this can happen, and put a plan in place to compensate for the downtime. For example, immediately after I completed the Boston Marathon, I couldn't escape the sense of "I haven't done anything with my life; I'm a total loser." To counter this, I put together a photo album of the marathon and started sharing my recent "win" with everyone so it would stay alive in my mind and help me remember that I wasn't a "loser."

Identifying Your Energy Rhythms

People with ADHD are often unaware of when their bodies are worn down. It's important to learn not only what types of projects create energy for you, but also which ones drain energy. That way, you can plan the most demanding activities during your peak energy times, as well as gauge when to stop working on a project and rest.

Keep a calendar or a log of your energy rhythms for a period of several weeks. This works best if the system is simple. For example, use a scale of plus or minus signs to depict high or low energy times, and write them beside different activities logged in a daily calendar.

Preplan for Bad Brain Days

Can't concentrate? Distracted? My clients call this a "bad brain day." For these days, it's important *not* to push yourself too hard and to have a failsafe plan in mind by knowing what works for you. Take a break and walk around the block, have a cup of tea, or call a friend. Then get back to work. One of my clients says he gives himself a "time-out" by going to a café near work to just "sit and chill" for an hour. The key is to know when these days hit and take action by doing what works for you.

Practice Relaxation Exercises

ADHD people often live in a state of constant stress. It's important to learn how to slow down and destress, both mentally and physically, at any given moment. Learn relaxation techniques and methods to center yourself at any given moment. Practice slow-breathing techniques or join a yoga or meditation class. If you are spiritual, make daily prayers a priority.

Take a Daily Inventory

Take time each day to reflect on your life and how you are living it. What do you want to change? What will it take? What are you willing to give up to get there? How were you of service today? How can you live a more purposeful life? Asking yourself these questions at the end of each day will help you focus on the things you can and cannot change in your life. That way, you can begin to focus more on the positive instead of the negative.

Give Thanks

One of my clients has made a habit of ending each day by writing down one thing for which she's grateful. She does this right before bed each night as a way of reflecting on the day she's just lived through and destressing before sleep. I've tried it, and I agree with her. It's amazing how you can learn to accentuate the positive!

PART IV

Living or Working with Someone with ADHD

"I wish you could talk to my family," I've heard from many clients.

I *have* talked to families, many of them. And I've listened, as well, to the spouses and children of my clients, to their partners or significant others, to those who are directly affected by the ADHD with which my clients cope. All of them have a stake in learning how to compensate for the symptoms that threaten to tear relationships apart, and what I hear over and over again is that they are willing to try almost anything to help their loved ones, if only they knew where to begin.

"I wish you could talk to my assistant or boss or coworkers," I've heard from clients, too.

The dynamics at work are different from those of the family, to be sure, but the investment each partner makes in a professional relationship is serious and important in its own right.

So I have talked to assistants and coworkers, to many people whose professional lives are closely entwined with those of my clients. I've also had the privilege of coaching them as part of the transition period when my clients leave our formal coaching relationship to put into practice all they've learned. At my clients' requests, I've taught these assistants about adjusting for their bosses' idiosyncrasies and ways of thinking and listened to survival stories from the trenches of their jobs. By tailoring strategies for accountability, structure, questioning, and listening to their unique situations, they've turned their working lives around.

Granted, I have experience and training and expertise in coaching individuals with ADHD, and I live each day as a woman with ADHD, so there's much I know and share about the subject. But what I've learned from all those to whom I've spoken—spouses, partners, children, assistants—also deserves to be shared, for they are the true experts, one might say, in surviving the nitty-gritty details there, where each story plays out. People and careers that they love are on the line, and in the necessity of the moment, they are doing what they must.

"It's been such a struggle to get this right, and we really have to make a commitment every single day," one client's wife told me. "I'd love to be able to help even one person by talking about what I'm learning."

"You have no idea how important this is," a client's assistant told me about my intention to include in this book real advice from real people affected by ADHD symptoms.

The families and colleagues of my clients have demonstrated insight, creativity, humor, and resilient goodwill in helping their loved ones and/or coworkers cope. They hope, along with me, that their comments and suggestions will help you, too.

CHAPTER 13

Loving Someone with ADHD, or, Did I Sign Up for This?

Brad ran through a litany of his wife's ADHD behavior when I asked him what living with her was like. "I have to prepare myself every time I walk in the house," he said immediately. "It's a perpetual soap opera. Will she be in tears because she hates herself today? Will she be laughing with a new best friend she just met at the market and dragged home? Will she even be home? Will there be smoke billowing from the kitchen from the latest dinner she's burned? Will there even be dinner?" He often felt worn down by the patience her unpredictability required. "It's hard not to lose it with her sometimes," he said, "if you know what I mean."

I do know. I've heard variations of his comments so often that I can almost write the script for them. "I communicate with him mostly by e-mail," was how the wife of one client put it. "I've given up on expecting him to sit and have a conversation with me. He just gets up and walks out of the room. I swear I see his back more than his face!"

Even children weigh in on their parents' ADHD. "I can understand how my parents got divorced," one teenager told me, "but not how they got married in the first place. My dad is so normal, but my mom is really crazy." He was talking about his mother's impulsive, distracted behavior, the way "she forgets things all the time, like me, even," and the toll it had taken on the entire family.

Fortunately, things don't have to be intolerable. If you live with an individual with ADHD, you don't have to "accept being constantly interrupted," as one husband complained, or "keep your comments short if you want to be understood," as another spouse remarked.

Families can learn to function, and function happily. Family members, like the ADHD individuals themselves, can educate themselves and create strategies for coping. In many ways, it comes down to understanding and to expectations.

"We used to fight a lot when I didn't think she was paying attention to what I was saying or when she went off in a million directions and forgot completely about the point of what we were discussing," I heard recently from a client's husband. "Now we've been communicating by instant message. It forces us both to focus and zero in on the issue we have to address. That way, she doesn't get so distracted. I wish I had thought of it a long time ago, it's made things so much easier."

Even though they can appear self-absorbed and can definitely be exasperating to others, I have yet to meet an individual with ADHD who wants it that way. "It's not like I'm trying to drive everyone crazy," I heard not too long ago. "Do they think I want to look stupid, like I can't retain information or understand what people are saying? Does anybody really think I don't want to be loved—or loving?"

The clients with whom I've worked don't want to use their ADHD as an excuse for inexcusable behavior, either. What they want is a way to work through the problems that their ADHD causes. "I'm sick of sounding so apologetic for everything about myself," a client told me. "It really makes me cry, too. There is a really serious issue with us that we are somehow bad and wrong and this is not to be tolerated or endured."

What my clients want is for family members to be there with them, everyone helping in whatever way possible to make the family unit strong. "My wife is totally supportive as much as she can be, and forgiving," said one client who, with his wife's help and commitment, had created a way to move forward after his diagnosis. "I don't play the ADHD card very often, like 'Honey don't expect this of me or that of me because this is my excuse.' You can't really get away with that anyway, which is good because you shouldn't."

But just as families of those with physical diseases or addictions need advice and support from others in similar circumstances, those living with partners with ADHD also need to know how others cope. It helps a woman to hear that she's not the only one living with a man who hyperfocuses at work but is too distracted elsewhere to buy a birthday card or show up on time for a dinner party. It helps a husband to know what other men do when their wives don't seem able to get organized or remember where they've promised to be.

Helpful Advice from Real Spouses and Partners

"People with ADHD always say that unless you have it yourself you can never really know what living with it is like," a client's wife told me. "Well," she went on, "the same thing is true for people who live with the people with ADHD. Believe me, somebody should ask us about that. We could help!"

Her comment underscored for me that it's one thing for me as the professional to offer advice to families about living with someone with ADHD, but it's quite another when suggestions come from those families themselves.

"All I can say is that for me, I tend to gather all the information and then try to make a clear decision about a path and tackle problems from every angle," one partner offered about the importance of learning about ADHD. "To that end, I am constantly pushing for diet changes and exercise and looking at a holistic route for helping my partner deal with his ADHD. I keep stressing the need for keeping to his medication schedule, because I can definitely see how important that is. He has a hard time seeing how all of these pieces fit together, but as long as I do, I find the strength to keep on trying to help, as long as he is receptive."

A client's wife brought up yet again the analogy of an additional child for whom she had to care. "I've told my husband before, it's like having another child. It's another person to manage and schedule because he frequently can't do it himself."

And it can also be scary. "When I see how much he is unable to deal with or manage at home," she said, "I wonder how he does it at work. I remember when he was first diagnosed—it was nice to have a label on what was a really tough time for us as a couple without even realizing the cause—I started to see a counselor to help me with the overload I was feeling. She said how it is really tough having a spouse in this situation because unlike a child, you can't just let them fail and learn from mistakes since those mistakes have major ramifications for the whole family. I think about that every time I'm trying to help him gain clarity in a situation, how I wish I didn't have to do that, but it is so necessary."

Knowledge and persistence, then, are crucial for spouses and significant others, as is flexibility. "I guess you have to throw out the idea of traditional roles," one husband said. "You have to accept the fact that you haven't married your mother, who stayed home and cleaned the house and baked pie and greeted your father at the door at six o'clock with a cocktail and a kiss. Your wife is just not that person, so please don't think she should be!"

Considering the lifestyle that so many of us experience, he could have been talking about almost any twenty-first-century woman, but this man made a good point about being married to someone with ADHD. You do need to change your expectations regarding traditional roles. There's more than a good chance that your wife won't be a good organizer, a perfect meal planner and shopper, a neat and tidy housekeeper, and a teacher/preacher/playmate to your children all at once. She's probably good at a lot of other things, though, so appreciate that and encourage her to develop her talents and interests. As one man said about his ADHD wife, "You have to love who she is, not who you expected her to be!"

The same holds true for women living with men with ADHD. "My father did everything around the house," one woman told me, "but my husband never gets around to repairs and things, so it's easier to hire somebody. Believe me, it saves a lot of hassles and arguing, so whatever it costs is worth it!" But she had to accept that about her husband and alter her expectations of the "man's" responsibilities.

A few couples have swapped traditional gender roles completely. "Look," I heard from a client's spouse, "I make a lot of money as a lawyer, and I'm good at my job. What he's good at doesn't pay a whole lot, but he happens to be a great cook and a great father. He loves to play, which he does with the twins, all day, every day, and when they're napping, he prepares dinner! So we're saving all the money we'd have to pay a live-in, plus we're keeping our privacy, and he's doing what he's good at and so am I when I go to the office. I hired a cleaning woman for the housework, and the arrangement works. Everybody's happy. All the tension we used to have is gone, at least in that area!"

One spouse's remarks really resonated with me. "I've done a lot of reading about this," he said, "and I know that ADHD doesn't begin only after you're married. I keep reminding myself that the woman I'm married to is the same one I fell in love with, the one I chose to spend my life with. That thought really helps me keep focused on what attracted me to her in the first place. It makes it easier to deal with the ADHD problems, and it helps me laugh the way I used to at how much she delighted me. I'm glad she keeps me on my toes!"

A few people ventured into the area of intimacy, a delicate subject for most. "My wife is so easily distracted that in the middle of the most intimate moments, she'll start talking about a phone call she forgot to make or a sale on furniture at Pottery Barn," someone told me.

"It's impossible to maintain any degree of intimacy then, and it got to the point that I thought we were in real trouble. But then we literally made rules, like having specific 'date nights' and 'no talking during sex.' I know that sounds crazy, but we kept trying to abide by the rules, and for some reason, it worked for us. Once we felt confident we could actually have some intimacy, we tried other things. I think it was basically about communicating what we each needed, which helped us be kinder to each other, even in the way we spoke to each other. This didn't happen overnight, mind you, but I want people to know you can get there."

Several partners commented on the tendency of mates with ADHD to become bored and their constant quests for new thrills. "In a way, I felt like we were teenagers sneaking around," a woman told me, "and I resented it. It seemed stupid. But that was something that actually excited him, so I tried not to see anything wrong with arranging nights at a motel once in a while, or other things even, to keep our relationship alive and exciting. I realized I had to work at this, which wasn't always easy since I was constantly annoyed at him for other things, like the way he always puts things off or forgets to call when he's going to be late. But I learned to compartmentalize and be happy about things we could make better, and intimacy definitely makes other things better, too."

So there you have it: real stories, real challenges, real ways of coping. With flexibility, creativity, imagination, intimacy, knowledge, persistence, laughter, and of course love, couples can lead satisfying and rich lives, even when one of the partners has

ADHD. As I heard from a former client's spouse, "What marriage or relationship doesn't have issues? ADHD can exaggerate or exacerbate things, but it doesn't have to spell the end of things. Commitment is commitment, period, and it's definitely worth the work!"

CHAPTER 14

Working for or with Someone with ADHD, or, Right-Brained Exec Needs Left-Brained Right Hand!

Most of my clients are highly educated professionals, and they're invested in demanding careers, so the impact of ADHD on their working lives is a topic I consider and discuss daily. I know their "wish lists" about how things might be.

"If only people in the office didn't assume that having ADHD means I'm clueless," a partner in a retail company told me. "They need to accept that I have certain ways of doing things that might be different from their own but that work for me. They should *not* simply try to impose their systems and styles on me, because that usually won't work at all. If I try to do things their way, I usually fail and I wind up feeling incompetent, and then things get totally messed up."

She could have been speaking for many of the clients I coach when she said, "I wish people could just reserve judgment more often and be curious about the way I do things. Sometimes they really need to pause and listen and think!"

On the other hand, those who work for my clients also have needs that must be considered, and they've given their perspectives, too.

Avoid Making Assumptions

"I've done a lot of reading about ADHD," an assistant to an executive with ADHD said. "A long time ago, my nephew was diagnosed, and I tried to learn as much as I could so I could understand him. When I began working for my boss, I could see some of the same patterns that my nephew showed, so I tried to ask questions about how he wanted things done and what I should do if he changed his mind midstream, things like that, the kinds of things my nephew needed us to do instead of getting impatient with him. Gradually, he began to trust me enough to open up about his ADHD, and we've worked out really specific ways of doing things to keep him focused."

But that assistant also admitted to making assumptions that didn't hold up. "I would definitely say that just because you might read about ADHD, it doesn't mean you know everything," she said. "You really can't assume anything."

She gave the following example. "My nephew was a reader, so maybe I didn't pay attention if the literature on ADHD said that people with it might not be readers. I used to bring my boss a lot of articles when he needed information or send him to different websites to read it online, but he didn't read the stuff. I had no idea what was going on. Finally we figured out a system that would work for us, but the key was communicating. Things changed only because he actually came right out and told me he won't read through lots of material. He said he couldn't wade through it all. That was a real revelation, and I knew we had to come up with some other plan."

She was grateful that her boss had moved past his embarrassment about a perceived weakness and had told her the truth. "So *assume nothing*," she said again. "Find out exactly what you're dealing with!"

Communicate Constantly

Other assistants also talked about the need for constant communication with bosses with ADHD, who are often erratic in their requests and demands.

It had been difficult, one said, to explain to her boss her own limits with his managing style. He couldn't keep throwing work at her at the last minute, for example, or keep changing his instructions for tasks. "Sometimes one task would change fifteen different times when I was in the middle of trying to complete it," she told me. "Now I know it was because he wasn't clear in his goals himself, but even so, it's impossible not to lose patience with somebody who does that. I guess the key is you can't take things personally, but I have to say, that's not so easy. I used to wonder if it was *me* who was messing up!"

Since individuals with ADHD often have trouble with time management, they can also have unrealistic expectations of what assistants or colleagues can accomplish in a given time period. "My boss would tell me he needed something in an hour that I'd really need at least three hours to do," I heard frequently.

"It took me a while to figure out why my boss kept expecting me to finish things in half the time they really took," one assistant said. "In the beginning, I honestly didn't think I'd survive. He's really bad at doing things on any kind of schedule, so he had no idea how much time an hour actually is. He'd give me way too much to do, and then I'd wind up frustrated and angry because I literally couldn't do the work, and then he'd wind up the same way because the work wasn't getting done. It was awful!"

She saw that she would have to speak up if she had any hope of remaining with him. "I would say it's important to meet on a weekly basis," she said, "and to be open and honest about both of your needs."

Be Aware of Your Language

One answer to many problems is effective communication.

Individuals with ADHD are usually hypersensitive to criticism, perhaps because they carry a history of disappointing others. Negative tapes echo constantly in their heads, and they hear every encounter as confirmation of past mistakes, which then triggers the pain those mistakes caused. Trying to hide their weaknesses, they're more likely to succumb to them when they feel judged, repeating the cycle they want desperately to escape.

On the other hand, they're usually "pleasers," so they're open to constructive feedback but shut down in the face of perceived anger. Nonjudgmental tone and word choice, as well as nonverbal communication and body language, are crucial in both personal and professional relationships.

"If we were going to make it as a team, I had to be truthful," a client's assistant said, "but I figured out I had to use nonthreatening language. I suppose I made faces or something, or rolled my eyes a lot when my superior would come marching in wanting to know, 'Where's the . . . I told you to do?' or, 'Who told you to do XYZ this way?' I could see how he would start to get anxious and angry, like I was criticizing him when I'd try to tell him that *he* did, *he* was the one who said, 'Do this, that, and the other thing,' but that now he's saying something different and changing his instructions."

She learned to have him write things down. "When he changed his mind," she said, "I'd show him his original goal and plan. Then I'd say something like 'Could you tell me how this fits in with what you wrote before?' or 'I want to be sure I do exactly what you're expecting me to do, so can you clarify if this means the same thing as that?' That way I didn't feel like I was being out of line, but I also wasn't letting myself be taken advantage of."

And her approach had unintended benefits. "You can actually

help develop some accountability and structure in your superior's interactions with you," she said, "if you keep in mind not to criticize, but to ask or suggest. It's like learning a whole new language, but guess what, it works with other people, too, like my husband. It's amazing how it stops people from getting defensive!"

She had also learned to state directly what she saw as the problem. "I realized that it was in both our interests for me to be up front, so I asked him bluntly if I could do that. I think I surprised him being blunt like that, but I promised that I wouldn't be mean or critical, just honest. I told him I wouldn't be super-stressed about his expectations then, and he could count on me to do exactly what he wanted. After a while, he actually began to think a little more about what he would say. It was right there in writing, so he couldn't act like he didn't say it."

Questions, Questions, Questions

"You have to keep your boss focused on priorities," one woman told me, which means asking lots of questions when he or she tries to put things off.

"He might tell you what his priorities are," she said, "and then when you sit down to do them, he'll stall and tell you, 'Oh, that's not really that important, we can wait on it.' So I absolutely have to check and double-check with him all the time. I'll say, 'You told me to remind you how important this is, so is there something you're avoiding? Is there something I can do to help you initiate the first step on it? What if we just spend five minutes talking about it right now?' That usually gets him to tackle whatever it is he's trying to avoid."

But it's important, she said, to be assertive, not aggressive, in your approach.

Try to Create Structure

"I need assistants who will take charge but not take over," one of my clients told me, "and those are two very different things."

Fortunately, there are assistants who know the difference.

"My boss will do anything to avoid structure," said a longtime assistant to a CEO. "It became one of my primary goals to keep him on track, so I always keep goals in front of him with visual timelines for all his projects. But I also keep reminding him verbally. And I never assume that he knows what's coming up!"

She also had to bring order to her boss's schedule, she said, so he would be realistic in planning. "In the beginning he'd be telling me to schedule appointments for him with so many different people, and then when it was time for him to keep the appointments, he'd have forgotten all about them and be involved with something else completely," she said. "I was new and I suppose rather timid, so I'd just try to cover for him with the people he was supposed to meet and say he had an emergency or something, and not get him upset by reminding him. Well, that didn't help anybody, because things kept sliding and a lot of people were getting very impatient and I was on the verge of a breakdown," she said. "And he seemed oblivious half the time!"

She had been close to resigning, she admitted, or perhaps to being fired, but she realized she should "fight for this job," as she put it. "I said to him one day that I really appreciated the opportunity to work for him, but that I needed to make sure that he followed through with commitments. I told him that I only wanted to set us both up for success, which was why I needed to speak out. And he appreciated it, and then we kept that kind of communication, and of course I kept my job!"

Patience

Almost every success story involves patience.

"I really need my assistants not to take my moodiness personally," said an investment banker with ADHD. "In fact, it's so important that they be really patient by nature that if they aren't, I'd say they shouldn't work for me or for anybody with ADHD. Chances are, if I act mad, I really am mad, but it's at myself for messing up. I have a hard time keeping in my frustration," he added, "and will most likely start to rant and rave, even swear. Believe me, it's not pleasant! It just means I feel like I've screwed up again. I have a history of screwing up, so when I do, I feel like I'm reliving every mistake I ever made in my life."

The best way for assistants to deal with this, he said, would be to just sit there quietly or ask him if they should take a short break. "They always used to think they had to answer me or explain themselves," he said, "so I had to hammer it into them that it was not them I was screaming at, it was myself. I think they were afraid to believe that."

Characterizing his behavior further, he said, "Some days I might come in and talk nonstop and do nothing but want to tell jokes, make everybody laugh, get them to lighten up. It's all a diversion from work, though, and I know that."

The best advice he could offer those working for someone with ADHD like him was to "listen to one or two jokes or stories, whatever we're telling, then say, 'Okay, let's get on track. You said you wanted to accomplish XYZ today.' We really need our assistants to give us structure since we don't have it ourselves, so when we go off like that, you have to jump in. We'll probably hate it and start swearing again, so be prepared for the fireworks, but we'll thank you later!"

Take Preventive Measures

Just as important, another assistant said, was to try to take pre-
ventive measures. "First you have to make sure your boss will let
you," she said. "I suppose that means that first your boss has to
be aware of what he does or doesn't do, and he also has to want
to change his ways. Otherwise you might get fired!"

She had a manager who frequently skipped their weekly meetings. "Decide in advance how to address the issue," she said. "Say
something like 'Remember we agreed that these meetings are
necessary. You told me that I need to remind you about this.' Ask
if you should place Post-it notes on his computer the day of the
scheduled meeting or beep him every fifteen minutes before it's
time. If you really want to get his attention," she added, "do what
I did once. I took his car keys so he couldn't leave the building
without seeing me first, and I got my meeting that way. He about
killed me, but he wound up thanking me later!"

Mutual accountability is really important, she added, "so make
sure you establish up front that part of your own responsibility is
to be vigilant in reminding your boss to do what he's supposed to
be doing."

Respect Boundaries

Most advice about respecting boundaries came not from assistants, but from those with ADHD themselves, who were quick to
acknowledge their own tendencies. "A lot of us with ADHD have
such low self-esteem that we think we need to make friends out
of everybody," one of my clients admitted. "But assistants can't
let us do that. They have to keep professional boundaries so they
can stay efficient."

Another client put it this way: "I need someone who will take
my work and me seriously and keep me focused. Sometimes I

actually sabotage my own success by trying to charm my assistants into hanging out instead of working. I need people around me who won't fall for that trap, so it takes a really strong individual to say to the boss, 'Excuse me, but let's focus on this task now.' But they need to," she said, repeating a familiar characterization, "because if we have ADHD, we need somebody else to keep the focus for us."

One client, a communications specialist with a home-based office, said something similar. "I told the people who work for me never to let me send them off on errands," he said, "or never let me tell them there's nothing for them to do today, so why don't they take a long lunch and come back tomorrow. If they ever left, I'd do nothing but screw around all day, maybe play computer games, check out real estate, anything. They should always check in on me to see if I'm doing my work, and if I tell them not to come into my office and to leave me alone, it means that I'm overwhelmed and have too much work to do. It's a warning sign to sit me down and ask me what I should be doing, or even what I'm avoiding."

Like so many other strategies assistants employ, however, a lot can depend on the ground rules that have already been established. One client warned, "You better not do anything too risky unless you and your boss have worked it out ahead of time. You can't just tell your boss to shape up and get to work if he didn't tell you that you could!"

Survival!

Individuals with ADHD usually have a good handle on the difficulties that working for them might present. "As a professional with ADHD, I've had over fifteen years of working with assistants, more of them than I'd like to admit," one executive said. "But each one has taught me something about myself and helped me to understand how to work with the next one, to the point where I almost have it down to a science—so much so that I've created a 'How to Work with Helen' cheat sheet!"

She had interviews preplanned. "When I hire someone," she explained, "I sit down with them and say, 'This is the best way for you to serve me.' Then I go through a list of how to handle a variety of situations. After I do this, I tell the person up front that if they don't feel comfortable doing some of the things I've requested, then we're not a right match and there's no point going further."

But if the match is right, the rewards can be well worth the effort. "Working for someone with ADHD can be fantastic," said an assistant to a college administrator. "Of course, that probably depends on that person's awareness of the label, and his interest and success in self-management. But working for Dr. H., I had a blast because he pushed my imagination to come up with practical solutions to complex problems. He saw connections that were not ordinary in business or life or education, and it forced me to see connections and find ways to exploit and harness those connections to create opportunities. I never got bored, never!"

Many people with ADHD are extremely creative, so the challenge for those who work with or for them is to be creative, too. "Some days my boss has what she calls 'bad brain days' when she can't think straight," an assistant told me. "If I see she's struggling that way, I remind her that on days like that she needs to take a break, so she'll go to yoga or go for a run or to the gym while I catch up on filing or other work. She loves snacks, so sometimes I just pull out the dried fruit or almonds. I guess it's a 'trust your gut' kind of thing, and food works great!"

There's frustration, to be sure, but there's also hope and fun. Longevity has its benefits when it comes to creative solutions. "After you've known your boss long enough—which means after that initial 'How am I ever going to last here!' shock wears off—you begin to feel more comfortable being as inventive as your boss actually is."

It can be really fun, she said, coming up with schemes and strategies to keep your boss in line. "Once I sent her on an errand for *me* just so I could get my part of the work done, and she had such a good time picking out a toy for my nephew that she was totally relaxed when she came back and we got everything done together that we needed to."

As difficult as their jobs might be, then, those who work for individuals with ADHD have opportunities for more "out of the

---

TIPS FROM A BOSS WITH ADHD ON HOW TO WORK WITH ASSISTANTS

- Meet on a weekly basis.
- Give permission for them to be vigilant in reminding you to do things.
- Be open and honest about your needs.
- Create accountability.
- Let go of details.
- Have them continually remind you of what you should be doing.
- Learn not to be ashamed of what you need.
- Be honest with yourself and with your helper.
- Give them permission to call you on the carpet.

TIPS FROM ASSISTANTS ON HOW TO WORK WITH BOSSES WITH ADHD

- Be clear with boundaries.
- Don't get caught up in their bad moods or overly excited moods.
- Ask them how they want to be reminded.
- If you ask them X and they say "no," just drop it. Nine times out of ten, it is just some emotionally irrational response. Give the boss time to think and then reapproach it.
- Stay calm and be honest at all times.

box" thinking and actual input than other superiors might allow. Take advantage of that situation, and let your imagination loose. Chances are good that your ADHD boss will appreciate it.

"To work for me, you'll need a sense of humor," said one, referring to where her disorganized mind sometimes leads her. "Take the work seriously, but a lot of things that happen here will seem really funny once we step back from them."

Then she added a life lesson for most situations. "Acknowledge and celebrate your differences," she said. "And don't be afraid to laugh!"

Final Thoughts

My friend and I are happy to share a number of interests in common, yet we delight all the while in our differences. She's been an avid reader all her life, but she never reads any self-help guides—"except for yours, Nancy!" as she's quick to point out. Neither she nor her husband has ADHD, but among the strategies she's read in my books and articles, "I always find things that I can apply to my own life," she says. "We're all just people first, so disability or not, we can all use tips on how to manage our lives."

She's also a reader and writer of poetry. I'm neither of those things, but I have read each of the poems she's sent me, and although I'm not always sure what her poems are saying, I do hear in each the voice of someone living a life she truly loves.

Several years ago, after returning from her morning run—a passion for both of us, I might add—she completed a poem she had been working on, called, appropriately enough, "Love Enough." It was about the passions of her particular life, but in the context of this book, I choose to believe that she could have been speaking for all of us when she wrote these lines:

I love that over and over
We start over,
That we stay in endless cycle—
I am, I have been, I shall be.

My sincere hope is that this book can become for you a way to start over, to leave behind the cycle of pain and discouragement your ADHD symptoms have caused, so that you can take control of your time, your tasks, and your talents.

May coaching, or self-coaching, enable you to begin again, now, a new habit of living a life you love.

May you believe with me that it's possible.

Afterword

by Sam Goldstein, Ph.D.

SALT LAKE CITY, UTAH

When we are no longer able to change a situation,
we are challenged to change ourselves.

—VIKTOR FRANKL

I have been evaluating and treating adults with attention deficit hyperactivity disorder since 1980, and over the years, I have been impressed with the challenges many adults with ADHD have overcome. I've learned that resiliency comes from developing a "can do" mind-set as well as from having someone who believes in you.

In our book, *The Power of Resilience,* Dr. Robert Brooks and I write that taking ownership of our behavior and becoming resilient requires the recognition that we are the authors of our lives. We must seek happiness not by asking someone else to change, but by asking instead what we can do differently.

Assuming personal control and responsibility is a fundamental underpinning of a resilient mind-set, one that affects all other features of this mind-set and serves as a catalyst to confront and deal effectively with problems. Resilient individuals find paths to become stress-hardy rather than stressed out. They are able to view life through the eyes of others, communicate effectively, and accept themselves and others. They are connected and compassionate, and they deal appropriately with mistakes. They focus on their assets and, most important, find ways to develop the self-discipline and self-control necessary to manage life's challenges.

Perhaps more than anything else, *The Disorganized Mind* resonates with me because of its framework of resilience. It is a book of life strategies that, while certainly beneficial for those with ADHD, could easily be marketed and offered as a guide for resilient living for everyone.

At the time I first met Nancy Ratey, I was about to author, with Ann Teeter Ellison, an edited volume on the assessment and treatment of adult ADHD. Our vision for this volume was not only to report the current science, but also to offer visionaries the opportunity to define their ideas, hypotheses, and suggestions for the future. Nancy Ratey was one such visionary, and in the chapter she contributed, she illustrated her concepts for coaching adults with ADHD. I found her model to be straightforward, empathetic, comprehensive, and consistent with what we knew about ADHD, cognitive psychology, and mind-sets.

Now Nancy Ratey has broken new ground and stretched the boundaries of the ADHD coaching field even further. From my perspective, this is the first comprehensive, self-help coaching volume for ADHD individuals. By explaining the foundation and tenets of coaching, and by offering guidelines to help readers understand when the assistance of others—a coach, therapist, or physician, for example—is needed, Ms. Ratey has provided an effective bridge between understanding her model and putting effective strategies into practice.

As baseball legend Gene Mauch said, "You can't lead anyone further than you have gone yourself." In her personal journey, Nancy Ratey has been to the moon and back. For adults with ADHD and those who live with and love them, this book is a treasured resource. It is a fully fueled shuttle on the launchpad, ready to help you live the life you want to live.

Index of Strategies

Following is a quick guide to locating strategies for the ADHD symptoms and issues addressed in this book:

ADHD Resources

ADHD Groups and Associations

Attention Deficit Disorder Association (ADDA)

15000 Commerce Parkway, Suite C
Mount Laurel, NJ 08054
Phone: 856-439-9099
Fax: 856-439-0525
www.add.org

Attention Deficit Disorder Resources

223 Tacoma Avenue South, #100
Tacoma, WA 98402
Phone: 253-759-5085
www.addresources.org

Children & Adults with ADHD (CHADD)

National Office
8181 Professional Place, Suite 150
Landover, MD 20785
Phone: 301-306-7070
Fax: 301-306-7090
www.chadd.org

A.D.D. Warehouse
300 Northwest 70th Avenue, Suite 102
Plantation, FL 33317
Phone: 800-233-9273
Fax: 954-792-8100
www.addwarehouse.org

ADD Consults
www.addconsults.com

ADD at About.Com
www.add.about.com

Attention Deficit Information Network
58 Prince Street
Needham, MA 02492
Phone: 781-455-9895

Association of Higher Education and Disability (AHEAD)
P.O. Box 540666
Waltham, MA 02454
Phone: 781-788-0003
Fax: 781-788-0033
www.ahead.org

Kitty Petty Institute
800 San Antonio Road, Suite 8
Palo Alto, CA 94303-4633
Phone: 650-855-9925
Fax: 650-855-9924
www.kpinst.org

National Center for Girls and Women with ADHD
3268 Arcadia Place NW
Washington, DC 20015
Phone: 888-238-8588
Fax: 202-966-1561
www.ncgiadd.org

Coaching Associations and Organizations

American Coaching Association
P.O. Box 353
Lafayette Hill, PA 19144
Phone: 610-825-8572
Fax: 610-825-4505
www.americoach.org

International Coach Federation (Not Strictly ADHD Related)
2365 Harrodsburg Road, Suite A325
Lexington, KY 40504
Phone: 888-423-3131 (toll-free); 859-219-3580
Fax: 859-226-4411
www.coachfederation.org

ADHD Coaches Organization
www.adhdcoaches.org

Institute for the Advancement of ADHD Coaching
www.adhdcoachinstitute.org

ADD Coach Academy
Slingerlands, NY 12159-9302
Phone: 518-482-3458
Fax: 518-482-1221
www.addca.com

Optimal Functioning Institute
Phone: 423-524-9549
Fax: 423-524-1239
www.addcoach.com

Coach University, Inc. (Not Strictly ADHD Related)
P.O. Box 512
Andover, KS 67002
Phone: 888-857-6410; 920-834-9663 (for callers outside of North America)
Fax: 1-888-857-6410
www.coachu.com

The Coaches Training Institute (Not Strictly ADHD Related)
4000 Civic Center Drive, Suite 500
San Rafael, CA 94903
Phone: 800-691-6008 (toll-free); 415-451-6000
Fax: 415-472-1204
www.thecoaches.com

ADHD Products and Services

ADD Audio Library—www.addaudiolibrary.com
ADD Consults—www.addconsults.com
ADD Classes—www.addclasses.com
ADD Resources—www.addresources.org
ADD Warehouse—www.addwarehouse.org
ADDitude Magazine—www.additudemag.com
ADDvance—www.addvance.com
ADDvisor—www.addvisor.com
Attention Research Update: Dr. David Rabiner—www.helpforadd.com
My ADD Store—www.myaddstore.com
National Resource Center for ADHD—www.help4adhd.org
ADD Articles—www.samgoldstein.com
ADD Research, Journal of Attention Disorders (www.sage.com/Journal of Attention Disorders)

Online ADHD Support Communities

ADD Community Center—www.addcommunitycenter.org
ADD Consults Chat—www.addconsults.com/digichat
ADD Forums—www.addforums.com
ADHD News Forum—www.adhdnews.com/forum

ADHD Blogs and Websites

ADHD.com
ADD@about.com—www.add.about.com
Adult ADD Strengths—www.adultaddstrengths.com
Adult ADD and Money—www.adultaddandmoney.com
ADD Coping Skills—www.addcopingskills.com
ADD Discussion Forum—www.sarisolden.com
Dr. Hallowell's Blog   www.drhallowellsblog.com
Focused Distractions—www.addconsults.com/blog
Living with ADD—www.livingwithadd.com
My ADD/ADHD Blog—www.myaddblog.com
Your ADD News—www.youraddnews.com

ADHD Experts

Russell Barkley—www.russellbarkley.org
Thomas Brown—www.drthomasebrown.com
Sam Goldstein—www.samgoldstein.com
Edward Hallowell—www.drhallowell.com
Thom Hartmann—www.thomhartmann.com
Kate Kelly—www.addcoaching.com
Terry Matlen—www.addconsults.com
Michele Novotni—www.michelenovotni.com
Patricia Quinn—www.addvance.com
John Ratey—www.johnratey.com
Nancy Ratey—www.nancyratey.com
Wendy Richardson—www.addandaddiction.com
Sari Solden—www.sarisolden.com

Job Accommodation and Resource Links

Job Accommodation Network—www.janwvu.edu
Job Application and the Americans with Disabilities Act—www.eeoc.gov
U.S. Equal Employment Opportunity Commission (EEOC)—www.eeoc.gov

Book List

Adler, Lenard, and Mari Florence. *Scattered Minds: Hope and Help for Adults with Attention Deficit Hyperactivity Disorder.* New York: Putnam, 2006.

Barkley, Russell A. *ADHD and the Nature of Self Control.* New York: New Guilford Press, 1997.

Brown, Thomas E., ed. *Attention Deficit Disorders and Comorbidities in Children, Adolescents, and Adults.* Arlington, VA: American Psychiatric Press, 2000.

Brown, Thomas E. *Attention Deficit Disorder: The Unfocused Mind in Children and Adults.* New Haven, CT: Yale University Press, 2006.

Conners, Keith and Juliette Jett. *Attention Deficit Hyperactivity Disorder (in Adults, Adolescents, and Children).* Kansas City, MO: Compact Clinicals, 1999.

Doyle, Brian B. *Understanding and Treating Adults with Attention Deficit Hyperactivity Disorder.* Arlington, VA: American Psychiatric Publishing, 2006.

Garber, Stephen W., Marianne D. Garber, and Robyn F. Spizman. *Beyond Ritalin: Facts About Medication and Other Strategies for Helping Children, Adolescents, and Adults with Attention Deficit Disorder.* New York: HarperPerennial, 1996.

Goldstein, Sam, and Anne T. Ellison. *Clinicians' Guide to Adult ADHD: Assessments and Intervention.* London: Academic Press, 2002.

Hallowell, Edward M., and John J. Ratey. *Answers to Distraction.* New York: Bantam Books, 1996.

———. *Driven to Distraction: Recognizing and Coping with Attention Deficit Disorder from Childhood Through Adulthood.* New York: Pantheon Books, 1994.

———. *Delivered from Distraction: Getting the Most Out of Life with Attention Deficit Disorder.* New York: Ballantine Books, 2005.

Hartmann, Thom. *Thom Hartmann's Complete Guide to ADHD: Help for Your Family at Home, School and Work.* Nevada City, CA: Underwood Books, 2000.

Kelly, Kate and Peggy Ramundo. *You Mean I'm Not Lazy, Stupid or Crazy?!: A Self-Help Book for Adults with Attention Deficit Disorder.* New York: Scribner's, 1995.

Kolberg, Judith and Kathleen Nadeau. *ADD-Friendly Ways to Organize Your Life.* New York: Brunner-Routledge, 2002.

Latham, Patricia H., Peter Latham, and Nancy A. Ratey. *Tales from the Work Place.* Washington, DC: JKL Communications, 1997.

Matlen, Terry. *Survival Tips for Women with Attention Deficit Disorder.* North Branch, MN: Specialty Press, 2005.

Murphy Kevin and Suzanne LeVert. *Out of the Fog: Treatment Options and Coping Strategies for Adult Attention Deficit Disorders.* New York: Hyperion, 1995.

Nadeau, Kathleen and Patricia Quinn. *Understanding Women with ADHD.* Bethesda, MD: Advantage Books, 2002.

Quinn, Patricia, Nancy A. Ratey, and Theresa Maitland. *Coaching College Students with ADHD: Issues & Answers.* Bethesda, MD: Advantage Books, 2001.

Ratey, John J. *A User's Guide to the Brain: Perception, Attention, and the Four Theaters of the Brain.* New York: Knopf Publishing Group, 2001.

———, and C. Johnson. *Shadow Syndromes: Recognizing and Coping with Hidden Psychological Disorders That Can Influence Your Behavior and Silently Determine the Course of Your Life.* New York: Pantheon Books, 1997.

Solden, Sari. *Journeys Through Adulthood.* New York: Walker & Co., 2002.

———. *Women with Attention Deficit Disorder,* 2nd ed., revised. Nevada City, CA: Underwood Books, 2005.

Weiss, Lynn. *The Attention Deficit Disorder in Adults Workbook.* Lanham, MD: Taylor Trade Publishing Company, 1994.

———. *Attention Deficit Disorder in Adults: A Different Way of Thinking,* 4th ed. Lanham, MD: Taylor Trade Publishing, 2005.

Young, Joel. *ADHD Grownup: Evaluation, Diagnosis, and Treatment of Adolescents and Adults.* New York: W. W. Norton, 2006.

Magazines

ADDitude Magazine—www.additudemag.com
Attention! Magazine—www.chadd.org

Index

About the Author

Nancy A. Ratey, Ed.M., M.C.C., S.C.A.C., is a strategic life coach who specializes in coaching high-achieving professionals with ADHD. She earned her master's degree in administration, planning, and social policy from the Harvard Graduate School of Education and is certified as a Master Certified Coach by the International Coach Federation and a Senior Certified Coach for the Institute for the Advancement for ADHD Coaching.

For the past two decades, Ms. Ratey has been actively coaching, teaching, and writing about her strategic coaching methodologies. She has coauthored two previous books, has written a home-study curriculum on ADHD for nurses, and has contributed to numerous lay and academic texts.

Known for her high energy and directedness, the author has served as president of the National Attention Deficit Disorder Association and has been on many advisory boards, including the Professional Advisory Board of Children and Adults with Attention Deficit Disorder.

As one of the founders of the ADHD coaching field, Nancy Ratey is internationally recognized as one of the foremost authorities on the topic. Her work has been featured in *The New York Times, Newsday, Wired,* and *Vogue* and on the ABC and CBS networks and National Public Radio.

Nancy Ratey currently practices in Wellesley, Massachusetts, where she resides with her husband, Dr. John J. Ratey.

For information and resources on ADD coaching,
visit the author's Web site:
www.nancyratey.com